DEC 2014

SWITZERLAND

ABDO
Publishing Company

SWITZERLAND

by Rebecca Rowell

Content Consultant
Clive Church
Emeritus Professor of European Studies
University of Kent

CREDITS

Published by ABDO Publishing Company, PO Box 398166, Minneapolis, MN 55439. Copyright © 2013 by Abdo Consulting Group, Inc. International copyrights reserved in all countries. No part of this book may be reproduced in any form without written permission from the publisher. The Essential Library™ is a trademark and logo of ABDO Publishing Company.

Printed in the United States of America,
North Mankato, Minnesota
102012
012013

Editor: Arnold Ringstad
Series Designer: Emily Love

About the Author: Rebecca Rowell has a Master of Arts in Publishing and Writing from Emerson College. She has edited numerous nonfiction children's books and written books for younger readers on a variety of topics, including Charles Lindbergh, Iraq, and natural gas. She visited Switzerland briefly several years ago and looks forward to returning.

Cataloging-in-Publication Data

Rowell, Rebecca.
 Switzerland / Rebecca Rowell.
   p. cm. -- (Countries of the world)
Includes bibliographical references and index.
ISBN 978-1-61783-638-1
1. Switzerland--Juvenile literature.   I. Title.
949.4--dc22

2012946081

Cover: The city of Interlaken

TABLE OF CONTENTS

CHAPTER 1
A VISIT TO SWITZERLAND

You begin next to a train station in Bern. The Church of the Holy Ghost, built in 1729, stands nearby. Looking toward the city, you see old cobblestone streets connecting an array of centuries-old buildings. You head east along one of the major streets, the Spitalgasse, to Piper Fountain. This sixteenth-century statue depicts a bagpiper dressed in red and blue. Continuing east, Spitalgasse becomes Marktgasse, the neighborhood's main street. Here you see a fountain dedicated to Anna Seiler, who founded the city's first hospital in 1354.

> **Switzerland lies entirely within a single time zone.**

This is Bern's Altstadt neighborhood. German for "old city," the Altstadt dates to the Middle Ages, and walking through it takes visitors back in time. The Altstadt has a large and varied collection of

Bern is the capital of Switzerland.

THE ALTSTADT'S CHILD EATER

Altstadt is home to fountains of all shapes and sizes. Some celebrate Bernese who lived centuries ago, while others feature fictional figures. The Child Eater Fountain is one example. Created in the 1540s by Hans Gieng, the fountain depicts a red and blue ogre eating a naked child. The child's head is in the ogre's mouth. Other children, stuffed in the ogre's bag and terrified, await the same fate. The reason for the design is unknown. Some speculate it was intended to frighten children in order to keep them away from a moat that was nearby, so they would not fall in and drown.

fountains, one of which honors Berchtold von Zähringen, founder of Bern.

POLITICAL AND CULTURAL CENTER

Next, you stop at the Federal Palace. Also located in the Altstadt, this is where Switzerland's parliament meets and the government works. Bern is the capital of Switzerland and the nation's political center. You notice people gathering at the palace's large fountain. Suddenly, its 26 jets—one for each Swiss canton, or state—erupt in a sort of water dance. People of all ages watch in delight, and some even stand in the water.

You sit down at a café and consider what else you'd like to do on your visit to Bern. Besides its political importance, Bern is also Switzerland's cultural center. Museums and art galleries abound. The new Paul Klee Center is one of the city's most popular museums. The building's wavelike shape is instantly recognizable. The museum is home to thousands of drawings and paintings by Klee, a celebrated Swiss artist who lived from 1879 to 1940.

To view a broader collection of artwork, you could walk across the Aar River to see the Museum of Fine Arts. Its holdings span several centuries and include paintings and sculptures by Swiss artists such as Ferdinand Hodler, Cuno Amiet, and Giovanni Giacometti. Some of Europe's greatest artists are represented as well, including Claude Monet and Vincent van Gogh.

Bern has several other museums, many of which focus on topics other than art. The Bern Historical Museum highlights the history of Bern and Switzerland. Other museums focus on subjects such as communication, natural history, and the Swiss Alps. Another famous attraction is the Bärengraben, or bear pit. Dating to the mid nineteenth century, the Bärengraben houses live bears, important symbols of the city of Bern. Though the bears can walk through a tunnel to the historic bear pit,

SWISS CANTONS

Cantons are the largest administrative divisions in Switzerland. They are similar to the states of the United States in that they have a high degree of independence, rather than being simple districts. Each canton has its own constitution and branches of government and handles matters that are not already assigned to the central federal government.

Political Boundaries of Switzerland

they mainly roam on an adjacent 65,000-square-foot (6,000 sq m) area of grassy land on the banks of the Aar River.[1]

MOUNTAINS WITHIN REACH

From your seat at the café you can see snowcapped mountains just miles away. You plan to explore these and other beautiful Swiss landscapes. Bern is surrounded by green, grassy hills dotted with quaint wooden chalets and farms. Cows stroll lazily in the fields of these farms, their bells clanking.

You can hike or bike Mount Gurten's trails. Bern's local mountain is only 30 minutes from the city's center. At the mountain you can also enjoy miniature golf, a miniature train, and ski and toboggan runs in winter. Mount Gurten offers amazing vistas, including panoramic views of Bern and of the famous snowy peaks of the Alps.

THE CLOCK TOWER

One of Bern's many attractions is the Clock Tower. The tower served as the city's western gate from 1191 to 1255 and is home to an astronomical calendar clock that was added in 1530.

The clock chimes four minutes before the hour, every hour of the day, as mechanical characters move. Bear cubs march, a rooster crows, and a jester presides over the scene.

CHEESE AND CHOCOLATE

Museums and mountains sound great, but right now you would prefer to get something to eat. Cheese is one of your favorite foods, which is good since Switzerland is known for fondue and raclette, two melted cheese dishes. They are typically offered at different cafés, so you find places to order both. Still a bit hungry, you might also try *rösti*, fried grated potatoes.

After your meal, you head back out to the streets of Bern. You pass a variety of shops. Watches and clocks decorate several shop windows, and you see many different models of the famous Swiss Army knife in glass cases. But chocolate is what you really want. The Swiss have a great reputation for it, and you do not have to walk far to find what you are looking for.

While strolling through Bern, you notice most signs are written in more than one language. People

SWISS CHOCOLATE

François-Louis Cailler was among the first Swiss chocolatiers. He began making chocolate in 1819 and invented a method to make chocolate bars. Daniel Peter of Vevy, Cailler's son-in-law, invented milk chocolate in approximately 1870 by adding powdered milk to chocolate paste. Other famous Swiss chocolate makers include Lindt, Nestlé, Sprüngli, and Teuscher.

Cows are a common sight on Swiss farms.

are speaking mostly Swiss German, but several are speaking French and Italian, too. There is another language that sometimes sounds like Italian, but you cannot figure out what it is. You are seeing and hearing the nation's four official languages: German, French, Italian, and Romansh.

SWITZERLAND'S GERMAN NAME

One of the German names for Switzerland, Schweizerische Eidgenossenschaft, does not translate to "Swiss Confederation." Instead, Eidgenossenschaft literally means "oath fellowship." The name refers to the legendary Rütli oath, a perhaps-legendary fourteenth-century agreement that was instrumental in the creation of Switzerland. A major figure in the event was the Swiss hero William Tell.

You are eager to see more of Switzerland. The nation is relatively small, but there is much to see and do. The country's regions are all within easy reach via an extensive rail network. Switzerland is roughly divided into different regions based on the dominant language used. Bern is in the German region.

You make plans to travel south to the famous Swiss Alps. You will ride the Jungfraubahn, a train which climbs the Alps to a height of 11,330 feet (3,454 m).[2] Here it stops at its final destination: Jungfraujoch, Europe's highest train station. There, you will see the spectacular Aletsch Glacier.

A street in the Swiss town of Stein am Rhein

But for now, you have another piece of chocolate and head back to your hotel. You want to get to bed early; you need your rest. There is a great deal of exploring to do.

NEUTRALITY AND PROSPERITY

Switzerland is more than just beautiful scenery and delicious cuisine. It also has a rich history, as well as remarkable political and economic systems. The country is equally well known for the success of its multiethnic and multilingual policies, and it is frequently regarded as having one of the highest standards of living in the world.

But Switzerland still faces a set of unique challenges. Its delicate environment leaves the country especially vulnerable to climate change. And with increasing international cooperation throughout the world, its isolationist stance and reluctance to join the European Union may leave Switzerland lagging behind in key areas.

Official name: Swiss Confederation, or Switzerland (in German, Schweizerische Eidgenossenschaft, or die Schweiz; in French, Confederation Suisse, or Suisse; in Italian, Confederazione Svizzera, or Svizzera; in Romansh, Confederaziun Svizra, or Svizra)

Capital city: Bern

Form of government: federal republic

Title of leaders: federal council (head of government and head of state)

Currency: Swiss franc

Population (July 2012 est.): 7,925,517
World rank: 96

Size: 15,917 square miles (41,277 sq km)
World rank: 136

Languages: German, French, Italian, and Romansh

Official religion: none, though individual cantons often have established churches

Per capita GDP (2011, US dollars): $43,400
World rank: 14

CHAPTER 2

GEOGRAPHY: LAND OF CONTRASTS

Switzerland is known for its natural beauty. Mountains dominate the landscape, covering most of the country. They have influenced the nation's history and shaped its identity. Though Switzerland is home to the Swiss Alps, the country's geography offers much more than that famous mountain range. Switzerland's varied landscape is a study in contrasts and includes beautiful lakes, verdant valleys, abundant plains, and lively cities.

LOCATION AND SIZE

Switzerland is located in the heart of Europe. It runs approximately 135 miles (220 km) from north to south and 220 miles (350 km) from east to west at its widest point.[1] The nation's total area is 15,917 square miles (41,277 sq km), nearly twice the size of New Jersey. Switzerland

Homes are nestled among Switzerland's many mountains.

ranks as the world's one hundred and thirty-sixth largest country.[2]

Switzerland's border totals 715 miles (1,852 km) in length.

Switzerland is a landlocked country, meaning it does not touch an ocean. The relatively small nation shares its borders with five other European nations: Germany to the north, Austria and Liechtenstein to the east, Italy to the south, and France to the west.

Switzerland has 26 cantons, each with its own capital. Major cities serve as centers for particular aspects of Switzerland: Bern is the nation's capital and political center; Basel is the industrial center; Geneva is the center of international organizations; and Zurich, Switzerland's largest city, is the economic center.

PEAKS AND VALLEYS

Switzerland has two major mountain ranges: the Alps and the Jura. The Swiss Alps are in the south and east, and they extend into France and Italy. Formed millions of years ago during a time of great geologic turmoil, then shaped further by glaciers, the Alps occupy almost two-thirds of Switzerland. Switzerland's highest peak is the Dufourspitze, the tallest summit of Monte Rosa, which spires to 15,203 feet (4,634 m).[3]

The Alps act as a barrier and can create weather variations in Switzerland.

The Swiss Alps are part of the large, discontinuous mountain chain known as the Alps. They reach through France, Italy, Switzerland, Germany, Austria, Slovenia, Croatia, Bosnia and Herzegovina, Montenegro, Serbia, and Albania. The Alps are approximately 750 miles (1,200 km) long, more than 125 miles (201 km) wide at their widest point, and cover more than 80,000 square miles (207,000 sq km).[4] In the Alps on the border between Switzerland and Italy sits the famous mountain known as the Matterhorn.

The Jura Mountains are in the north and west, forming a 225-mile (360 km) arc between Switzerland and France.[5] Most of the Jura range lies in Switzerland, occupying approximately one-eighth of the country. These mountains were formed in the same way and at the same time the Alps were formed. However, glaciers eroded the Jura

THE MATTERHORN

The Matterhorn is known around the world. The name translates roughly to "the peak in the meadows." This famous peak reaches 14,692 feet (4,478 m) and straddles the border between Switzerland and Italy.[6] To the Swiss, the Matterhorn appears to be a stand-alone peak, but it is actually the end of a ridge. The slope of the Swiss side is less steep than the slope of the Italian side. This difference in slope led to a successful climb of the Matterhorn via the Swiss side in 1865. Many climbers had tried unsuccessfully to ascend the mountain from the Italian side before Britain's Edward Whymper completed the climb on the Swiss side on July 14, 1865. The descent was not as successful—four members of his party fell to their deaths. Just three days after Whymper reached the top, climbers succeeded in ascending the Matterhorn from the Italian side. People continue to climb the mountain today, often in summer.

even more, leaving them smaller than the Alps. The Jura's highest Swiss peak, Mont Tendre, surpasses 5,500 feet (1,680 m), making it considerably smaller than the Dufourspitze.[7]

Jura is Celtic for "forest," aptly describing the range, which is blanketed with thick forests. The name is also related to the Slavic word *gora*, or "mountain." The mountains lend their name to the Jurassic Period, an era from which many fossils have been discovered in the area.

SWISS PLATEAU

Between Switzerland's two mountain ranges lies a very different landscape: the Mittelland, or middle land. This region occupies almost one-third of Switzerland, stretching from Lake Geneva in the southwest, on the French border, to Lake Constance in the northeast, on the German and Austrian borders.

The Mittelland is a plateau with rolling, fertile landscapes. Two-thirds of

SAINT GOTTHARD PASS

For centuries, crossing the Alps was dangerous. The passage was made somewhat safer by the construction of the first bridge over Saint Gotthard Pass in the thirteenth century. The pass is located at an elevation of 6,916 feet (2,108 m). Artifacts, including gold jewelry dating to the fourth century BCE, have been discovered at the site. Archaeologists believe they were given as offerings for safe passage through the treacherous terrain. The pass is 16 miles (26 km) long.[8]

Today, the area has a modern road. Saint Gotthard Tunnel was constructed underneath the pass for trains by 1882. A road tunnel was built in 1980, and a new tunnel for trains was started in 2010, to be dug below the current tunnels. It will run for 35 miles (57 km) and is scheduled to begin service in 2017.[9]

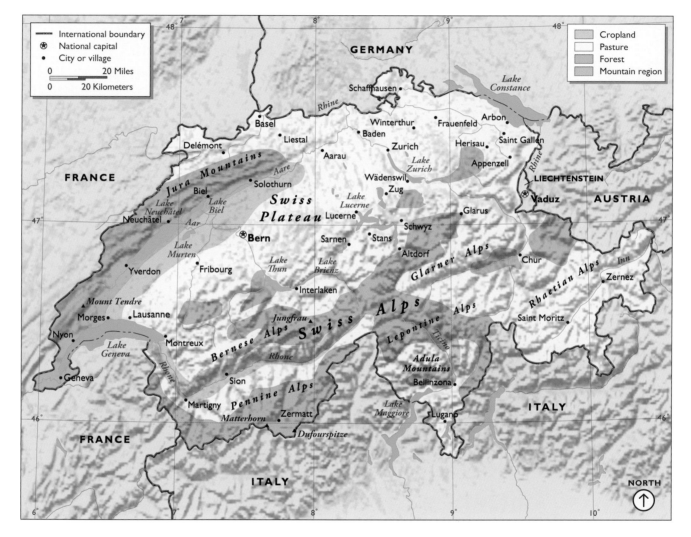

Geography of Switzerland

the Swiss population, along with industries and farms, are located here. The area is one of the most densely populated in Europe, with an average of 1,166 people per square mile (450 people per sq km).[10] The lowest and flattest part is the district around the three western lakes: Biel, Murten, and Neuchâtel.

RIVERS AND LAKES

The lakes that bookend the Mittelland—Geneva and Constance—are the nation's largest. Six percent of Europe's freshwater is in Switzerland; the country contains more than 1,500 lakes.[11] Other major lakes include Lucerne and Zurich. With an area of 84 square miles (218 sq km), Neuchâtel is the largest Swiss lake entirely within the nation's borders.[12]

Switzerland is also home to numerous rivers and streams. Two of Europe's greatest rivers, the Rhone and the Rhine, begin in Switzerland. The Rhone flows west into Lake Geneva and then into France. The Rhine flows east into Lake Constance and then turns west, forming the border between Switzerland and Germany. The Rhone, Rhine, Inn, and Ticino Rivers have helped to define the Swiss landscape, carving deep valleys that lie in stark contrast to the soaring peaks of Switzerland's mountains. Each of these rivers flows into a different sea: the Rhone to the Mediterranean Sea, the Rhine to the North Sea, the Inn to the Black Sea, and the Ticino to the Adriatic Sea.

Swiss lakes cover a combined area of approximately 521 square miles (1,349 sq km).

CLIMATE AND SEASONS

Four distinct European climates converge in Switzerland. Cold, dry air comes from the north, while warm, moist air comes from the south. The west sends moist, mild air, and the east sends warm air in summer and cold, dry air in winter.

Generally, Switzerland's climate is temperate, though it varies greatly depending on location. Altitude plays a major role, with temperatures decreasing as altitude increases. Winter is usually cold and cloudy, with rain and snow. Summer varies from cool to warm.

Climate can also vary greatly within a short distance, especially when altitude changes. The city of Saint Gallen and the Säntis, a mountain, are approximately 12 miles (19 km) apart. Saint Gallen has an elevation of 2,556 feet (779 m) and averages 50 inches (127 cm) of precipitation annually, while the Säntis, which reaches 8,202 feet (2,500 m), averages more than 110 inches (279 cm) of precipitation annually.[13]

The Monch (Monk) Mountain stands at 13,448 feet (4,099 m) and averages 163 inches (414 cm) of precipitation per year, the most in the nation. The town of Stalden, located in a valley in southern Switzerland, has the lowest average precipitation at 21 inches (53 cm).[14]

The Alps are an important factor in Swiss climate. They act as a barrier, so the weather in the north is often quite different from that in the south. Winters are noticeably milder in the south than in the north.

A boat sits just offshore on Lake Geneva, Switzerland's largest lake.

Switzerland has four distinct seasons. Spring lasts from March to May and is a time of rebirth, when plants come to life. Summer is the warmest season and lasts from June through August. Autumn lasts from

AVERAGE TEMPERATURE AND PRECIPITATION

Region (City)	Average January Temperature Minimum/Maximum	Average July Temperature Minimum/Maximum	Average Precipitation January/July
The Mittelland (Zurich)	29/36°F (–2/2°C)	58/73°F (14/23°C)	2.4/5 inches (6.1/12.7 cm)
The Alps (Zermatt)	17/29°F (–8/–2°C)	51/66°F (11/19°C)	1.6/2.2 inches (4.1/5.6 cm)
Geneva (Geneva)	29/39°F (–2/4°C)	56/77°F (13/25°C)	2.2/2.8 inches (5.6/7.1 cm)[15]

September to November. Fruits, vegetables, and crops are harvested at this time. Winter is December through February; during this time, much of the land is blanketed with snow.

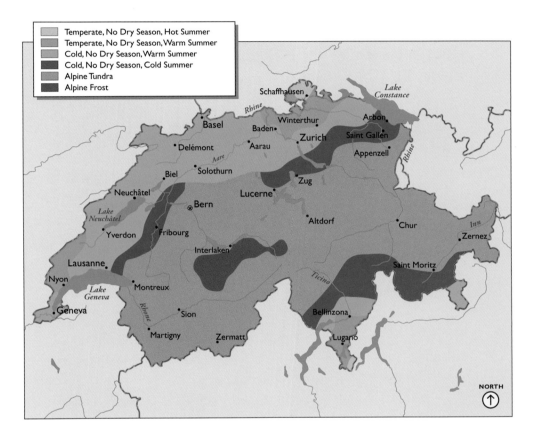

Legend:
- Temperate, No Dry Season, Hot Summer
- Temperate, No Dry Season, Warm Summer
- Cold, No Dry Season, Warm Summer
- Cold, No Dry Season, Cold Summer
- Alpine Tundra
- Alpine Frost

Schaffhausen

Lake Constance

Rhine

Basel

Winterthur

Arbon

Baden

Zurich

Saint Gallen

Delémont

Aarau

Appenzell

Aare

Biel

Solothurn

Rhine

Neuchâtel

Zug

Lucerne

Lake Neuchâtel

⊛ Bern

Altdorf

Chur

Inn

Yverdon

Fribourg

Zernez

Interlaken

Lausanne

Saint Moritz

Nyon

Ticino

Lake Geneva

Montreux

Geneva

Bellinzona

Sion

Rhone

Martigny

Zermatt

Lugano

NORTH
↑

Climate of Switzerland

CHAPTER 3

ANIMALS AND NATURE: ALPINE WILDLIFE

Switzerland is home to an estimated 50,000 species of plants and animals.[1] Most of these are plants. Trees populate thousands of acres of forest, while valleys are covered with grass and wildflowers. Shimmering lakes dot the land. All of these areas are inhabited by a wide assortment of wildlife, including some that are present due to human intervention.

REINTRODUCING THE IBEX

Ibex, goats with long, curved antlers, can be spotted on Alpine mountainsides, but that has not always been the case. Though the ibex was once plentiful in Switzerland, people eventually began using its body

The agile ibex is able to traverse Switzerland's mountainous terrain.

parts to create traditional cures for a variety of diseases. As a result, the ibex was hunted to near extinction in the early nineteenth century.

The ibex was returned to Switzerland in the early twentieth century. The animal was reintroduced to the Swiss National Park, located in the eastern canton of Graubünden, between 1920 and 1934. Additional herds of ibex live in the cantons of Bern and Valais. Today, approximately 15,000 ibex live in Switzerland.[2]

ALPINE SALAMANDER

The alpine salamander has adapted to survive in the high altitudes of the Alps. This amphibian lives in areas with elevations as high as 10,000 feet (3,000 m).[3] It is the only European amphibian that gives birth to live young, and the gestation period for mother salamanders living above 4,600 feet (1,400 m) may be as long as three years. These adaptations make these salamanders' offspring less susceptible to predators than the eggs laid by most salamander species.

ALPINE ANIMALS

Other animals common in the mountains are chamois, marmots, badgers, deer, foxes, rabbits, and squirrels. Lizards and snakes are located primarily in the southern region, and many varieties of insects exist throughout Switzerland.

Switzerland's bird population includes the

The alpine salamander grows to a length of approximately six inches (16 cm).

golden eagle and lammergeier, or bearded vulture; both are found in the southeast. Black Alpine choughs, rock ptarmigans, nutcrackers, and grouse are also common in Switzerland.

A handful of fish species inhabit Switzerland's lakes and rivers. Varieties include carp, grayling, perch, and whitefish. There are two varieties of trout: lake and brook. Trout are popular among fishermen, though not as plentiful as they once were.

FORESTS, MEADOWS, AND ICE

Almost one-third of Switzerland is forested. The Jura are covered with dense forests, and the Alps have three altitude zones that have different types of flora. In the lowest zone, deciduous forests of beech and oak grow at elevations as great as 4,264 feet (1,300 m) and coniferous forests that include the larch and arolla, or Swiss pine, grow at altitudes up to 6,232 feet (1,900 m).[4] The middle zone, located above the trees, has bushes, scrub, and grassy meadows with wildflowers. The highest zone is glacial. It has a permanent covering of snow and ice.

Wildflowers abound in Switzerland's meadows from April to July. Their brilliant shades of blue, yellow, and pink color the landscape. Crocuses and gentians appear in spring, followed by alpine orchids, glacier buttercups, miniature rhododendrons, and rock jasmine. Switzerland's

Trees and meadows give way to glacial areas at higher elevations.

national flower is the edelweiss. It is Alpine as well, growing at altitudes of up to 10,170 feet (3,100 m).[5]

ENVIRONMENTAL THREATS

Switzerland's natural resources are being threatened by multiple factors. Climate change is altering Switzerland's mountains: warmer temperatures have caused its glaciers to melt, losing approximately one-third of their surface area and one-half of their density between 1850 and 1970.[6] Shrinking glaciers continue to affect flora, fauna, people, and the economy. Added water from glacier melt may lead to floods and landslides. Over time, the loss of glaciers will likely affect the rivers they supply, such as the Rhone. This will in turn affect the Swiss hydroelectric system, winter sports tourism, and farming.

INVASIVE PLANTS AND ANIMALS

Switzerland is struggling with exotic plants and animals that are threatening native species by competing for habitat. Some also carry diseases that kill off native species, and some are toxic to humans. One example is the giant hogweed, native to Asia and the Caucasus. It erodes riverbanks and its sap can cause skin to burn and blister.

The American grey squirrel is an invasive animal species. It entered the country through Italy and is expected to destroy Switzerland's native squirrel population if something is not done to intervene. Some invasive species are brought in knowingly, while others have been accidentally introduced to Switzerland.

Higher temperatures also change the landscape. A 1.8 degree Fahrenheit (1°C) increase causes the tree line to move up 330 feet (100 m).[7] The mountain habitat changes as some plants and animals move up the mountain and others die out. Some mountains have more plant species than they did 100 years ago, while some species no longer exist. As the vegetation changes, certain animals suffer. The mountain hare is one example. The animal's habitat is decreasing; as a result, hare populations are becoming separated, making breeding difficult.

Urbanization is also threatening Switzerland's ecosystems. Humans continue to overtake the

ENDANGERED SPECIES IN SWITZERLAND

According to the International Union for Conservation of Nature (IUCN), Switzerland is home to the following numbers of species that are categorized by the organization as Critically Endangered, Endangered, or Vulnerable:

Mammals	2
Birds	1
Reptiles	0
Amphibians	1
Fishes	9
Mollusks	9
Other Invertebrates	28
Plants	5
Total	55[8]

landscape, including farmland. And from 1984 to 1995, only one tree was planted for every four removed.[9] Pollution has been another result of urbanization. Most air pollution is the result of vehicle and industry emissions. Changes in industry have lessened pollution in the last 20 years, but an increased number of cars and trucks on Swiss roads has offset those gains.

Groundwater, the source of approximately 80 percent of drinking water in Switzerland, is also polluted.[10] Agriculture is the biggest contributor to this problem due to its use of pesticides that seep into the ground. Fertilizer and leaking sewage lines also contribute. Acid rain, another type of pollution, has proven devastating to mountain trees. An estimated 40 percent of these trees are sick, damaged, or dying.[11] Trees serve as homes for animals, help maintain the landscape, and are natural avalanche barriers, so their decline is problematic.

ENVIRONMENTAL CONSERVATION AND PRESERVATION

Over the last 150 years, more than 220 species of plants and animals have disappeared from Switzerland.[12] In response to this and other environmental threats, the Swiss government established laws in the 1970s and 1980s to help preserve Switzerland's natural beauty.

A worker collects eels killed by a chemical spill in the Rhine River in 1986.

INFO
Bär

Sicherheits-
hinweise!

Wenn sie den Bär
sehen, bleiben sie
bitte auf der Strasse
und versuchen sie
nicht, sich dem Bär
zu nähern !

The Swiss National Park was formed in 1914 and was instrumental in reintroducing the ibex to Switzerland. There are also many other protected areas throughout the country. Organizations such as the Swiss Foundation for the Protection of the Countryside and the Swiss Landscape Fund focus on maintaining and improving Switzerland's environment.

Awareness of environmental threats has resulted in the establishment of such parks as the Swiss National Park.

CHAPTER 4
HISTORY: STRENGTH IN UNITY

Prehistoric people first lived in Switzerland as long as 150,000 years ago. Neanderthal hunters, closely related to modern humans, had established settlements by approximately 50,000 BCE. Homo sapiens, or modern humans, were in Switzerland by approximately 12,000 BCE, arriving during a period of glaciation. After the glaciers subsided, Neolithic peoples using stone tools grew crops and bred animals in the Rhine and Rhone valleys by approximately 5000 BCE. More than 3,000 years later, in approximately 1800 BCE, people settled in the valleys of the Alps and the Swiss plateau.

Switzerland's mountainous terrain meant that early settlers had to carefully plan which routes to take when migrating into the area.

THE SWISS GUARD

Swiss mercenaries had a reputation for being outstanding soldiers. The Roman orator Tacitus (56–120) described them thusly: "The Helvetians are a people of warriors, famous for the valour of their soldiers."[1] Swiss mercenaries served many European royals, notably in France and Spain.

On January 22, 1506, 150 Swiss guards began serving at the Vatican, pledging allegiance to the pope. Swiss Guards have served the pope ever since. Today, the guard has 100 members: one commander, three additional high-ranking officers, 23 lesser officers, 70 pikemen, two drummers, and one chaplain.[2] The Swiss Guard is known for its ceremonial uniform, which was designed in the early twentieth century but which echoes Renaissance-era fashions. It has bold vertical stripes of blue and yellow, red accents, and a high, white, ruffled collar. Ostrich feathers adorn the top of the helmet, their colors signifying rank.

THE CELTS AND ROMANS

The Celts were a European people who lived in central Europe as early as 700 BCE. A Celtic tribe known as the Helvetians settled in what is now western Switzerland by the second century BCE. The Helvetians were a powerful tribe, skilled at ceramics and metalwork, and they held much of the Swiss plateau. Another group, the Rhaetians, settled in the east. It is believed they are related to the Etruscans, who lived in what is now the Tuscany region of Italy.

German tribes pushed the Helvetians into Switzerland and continued to threaten the Celtic group. In 58 BCE, the Helvetians headed west, planning to move into Gaul (now France and Belgium). The area was occupied by Romans. Julius Caesar, the Roman governor, turned away the Helvetians. He and his troops then defeated the Helvetians in Bibracte. The Helvetian survivors returned to live under Roman rule.

In 15 BCE, Roman troops conquered the Rhaetians, and the rest of what is now Switzerland was added to the Roman Empire. The Romans built on top of several Celtic settlements and also created new cities, primarily on lakeshores. Basel, Chur, Geneva, Lausanne, and Zurich are all former Roman settlements. Under Roman rule, Switzerland was split into five provinces. The Romans improved water supplies and roads, and built arenas, theaters, schools, and farmsteads. They introduced a variety of plants, vegetables, and fruits to the country, including grapes. Latin, the language of the Romans, became the official language.

FOREIGN RULE

Germanic tribes first raided Roman-controlled Switzerland in 259–260 CE. By 400, the tribes—primarily the Alemannians and Burgundians—occupied the east and west of modern Switzerland. By the early sixth century, the Franks, another Germanic tribe, conquered the whole of the country and made it part of a larger empire.

The Latin form of Switzerland's name—Confoederatio Helvetica—honors the Helvetians who settled the area.

The Romans had introduced Christianity, which spread. Over the centuries, as churches and monasteries were built, the Catholic Church owned increasing amounts of land and controlled the people living on it.

By the ninth century, Switzerland was part of the Holy Roman Empire, governed by Charlemagne. He ruled through the noble families who had emerged and would continue to grow in power.

Charlemagne died in 814. In 843, his empire was divided among his grandsons. During the ninth and tenth centuries, foreigners invaded. The Muslim Saracens briefly invaded the south and west, while Hungarians destroyed monasteries and the city of Basel.

The pieces of Switzerland were reunited under the rule of the Holy Roman Empire by German emperor Conrad II in 1032. Local rule varied. An area might be controlled by a noble family, a non-noble lord, an abbot, or a bishop, all of whom held varying degrees of power.

Feudal dynasties eventually took control. The Zähringen, Savoy, Kyburg, and Habsburg families each founded cities and monasteries in the lands that became Switzerland. Farming improved, prosperity increased, and people became traders and craftsmen. The opening of the Saint Gotthard Pass, providing a direct route to the rich cities of northern Italy, boosted trade. Urban areas developed. Some places, such as Uri and Schwyz, were given imperial freedom. Only the emperor, no longer a local ruler, governed these cantons. Over time, additional cantons were granted such independence.

THE CANTONS UNITE

In 1273, Rudolph I, a member of the royal German Habsburg family,
became emperor of the Holy Roman Empire. He ruled harshly, taxed
heavily, and died in 1291. Fearing new troubles, the Swiss saw a need
to unite to ensure their independence. Communities allied with one

another. In the Rütli meadow, near Lake Lucerne, the Uri, Schwyz, and Unterwalden cantons formed the League of the Three Forest Cantons by swearing to mutually defend their liberties. The agreement was enshrined in a charter and is seen as marking the beginning of what would eventually become Switzerland.

The armies of the three cantons joined to defeat a Habsburg army in 1315. Following this victory, the alliance was renewed with a more ambitious Federal Charter. Because men from canton Schwyz were prominent in the battle, outsiders began calling all the confederates Schwyzers or Switzers, and their confederation Schweiz or Suisse. The confederation grew over the next 200 years as other communities pledged their allegiance. When the Habsburgs tried to force the canton of Lucerne to fight the confederation in 1332, it joined the Schwyzers instead.

The confederation's army became a major force in Europe, helping to destroy the powerful Duchy of Burgundy and acquiring new lands in Italy. In 1499, the Swiss won independence from the Holy Roman Empire in the Swabian War. However, in 1515, the divided Swiss army was defeated in the Battle of Marignano, overcome by a combined force of French and Venetian troops with stronger artillery and cavalry.

The event marked the end of Swiss expansion and the beginning of Swiss neutrality. Swiss troops no longer fought for the confederacy,

Though the Swabian War lasted only months, its result had a lasting impact on Swiss history.

but rather as mercenaries, which brought them much needed money during a time of great poverty. The confederation continued to grow with alliances and the addition of new communities and conquered territories. By 1513, it included 13 cantons and other territories, and by the late fourteenth century it had its own diet, or parliament.

REFORMATION

The sixteenth century marked the beginning of the Reformation, a time of religious upheaval in which Protestants rejected the pope and the Catholic Church. The Reformation became more than a religious conflict. It was a challenge to much of the region's existing social structure, adding to the destruction that occurred during this period.

Two of the movement's leaders were in Switzerland. Huldrych Zwingli, a priest, led reforms in German-speaking Zurich in 1523. He died in a civil war against Catholic forces in 1531, but the Reformation continued. A Frenchman named John Calvin began leading the Reformation in French-speaking Geneva in 1536. Catholics launched a counterreform in 1545. Some cantons remained Catholic, while others were Protestant. Canton Appenzell ultimately split into two half cantons: one Catholic, one Protestant.

John Calvin, a major figure in the Reformation, worked in Geneva.

SEVENTEENTH AND EIGHTEENTH CENTURIES

European religious and territorial battles continued in the seventeenth century with the Thirty Years' War (1618–1648). The war was fought in different parts of Europe, but primarily in Germany. The lengthy conflict affirmed the importance of unity to the Swiss—differences aside, staying together and staying out of the lengthy war was deemed best for the confederation.

The Swiss also decided to defend their borders during this time. Protestant troops from abroad violated the confederation many times by entering Swiss territory. A joint military council of Catholics and Protestants was formed in 1647, ensuring that 36,000 troops would defend the confederacy's border if necessary.[3]

The Thirty Years' War affected the confederation in another way. Switzerland did not fight in the conflict, but it was an integral part of the agreement that ended the war. As part of the 1648 Treaty of Westphalia, the Swiss confederation was for the first time formally recognized as being wholly independent by the major European powers.

The eighteenth century was generally peaceful and prosperous for the Swiss. Agricultural output increased and clockmaking and textiles started as home industries. Workers made clocks and textiles such as

A painting depicts the signing of the Treaty of Westphalia.

lace at home using tools and supplies from business owners. Textiles were part of the slave trade, exchanged for enslaved Africans who were then sold in the Americas. Bankers who financed European governments and overseas trade benefitted, too.

Swiss society became prosperous but very conservative, with power and privilege restricted to a small group of elites. This was challenged by a variety of social groups, some of them patriotic. The Helvetic Society was created in 1762, bringing together Swiss from across the confederation in support of reform and unity, despite their religious and linguistic differences.

FRENCH OCCUPATION

The end of the eighteenth century brought great change. The French Revolution began in 1789 and its ideas had a significant effect on Switzerland. Some Swiss were encouraged to seek change in their home country. Others were frightened by the revolution, especially after August 1792, when many Swiss mercenaries serving as guards to the king of France were massacred.

France temporarily annexed several cantons during its rule over Switzerland.

France, desiring Switzerland as a buffer zone and for its resources, invaded in 1797. With the support of Swiss revolutionaries, the French reorganized the confederation into one centralized state, the Helvetic Republic. It had a constitution and a central government, and cantons were deprived of much of their autonomy, ignoring their historical roles. Subjection to France also required Switzerland to act as an ally and provide France with soldiers, which ended its long-held neutrality. For the next 16 years, as the French battled their European neighbors, Switzerland felt the effects of war.

The new government also suffered from infighting; many Catholic conservatives rejected the changed order and the revolutionaries were themselves divided. So, in 1803, French leader Napoléon I largely restored the former system of cantons and added six to their number. A new constitution was instituted that restored Switzerland's official neutral stance, though the Swiss had to continue supplying troops to France.

BECOMING A FEDERAL STATE

Napoléon's empire finally went into decline following its defeat in Russia in 1812. In 1813, opponents of the revolution attempted to restore the old political and social structures in Switzerland. Instead, a new compromise confederation was established, with three new cantons.

The country remained very divided between those who wanted change and those who did not. Those who did not were largely Catholics. In 1830, more than half the cantons added liberal and democratic elements to their constitutions, but they were unable to change the national constitution. Relations between the two sides worsened, and there were violent attacks on the Catholic cantons. Seven conservative cantons united to form the Sonderbund, or separatist

"SWISS PSALM"

Switzerland's national anthem is the "Schweizerpsalm," or "Swiss Psalm." Leonhard Widmer wrote the German lyrics in 1841 and sent the poem to composer Alberik Zwyssig to set to music. Zwyssig chose a hymn he had composed for an ordination service in 1835. The "Swiss Psalm" became the provisional Swiss anthem in 1961, replacing the unofficial anthem "Are You Calling, My Fatherland." "Swiss Psalm" became the official anthem in 1981.

league. The Parliament declared the Sonderbund illegal in 1847, and won a decisive victory in the brief Sonderbund War of November 1847. In 1848, the confederation, now led by forces who sought change, drafted a new constitution. Twenty-two cantons approved it, creating a federal state with a bicameral legislature, a federal supreme court, and a seven-member government with a rotating presidency. The constitution also specified several civil rights for citizens, including voting for men. The Swiss nation state was born.

Switzerland flourished in the latter half of the nineteenth century. Neutrality was at the center of its foreign policy, which focused on humanitarian work. The organization later known as the Red Cross was founded in Switzerland in 1863. Political parties developed and found that the new political system had room for all, including those who had

Zurich in the 1880s

supported the Sonderbund. The Swiss constitution was amended in 1874. Basic education was made mandatory for all youth; primary schooling was provided free of charge and without church interference. Direct democracy expanded. With sufficient demand from citizens, any proposed new laws could be put on a nationwide ballot. More aspects of the government were centralized, including the military.

At the same time, industrialization continued. The chemistry and machine-tool industries emerged. Industrialization improved agricultural production, though this resulted in a great reduction in the need for workers. Out-of-work farmers moved to the towns or simply emigrated. Roads were improved and the railroad was introduced, launching the tourism

THE RED CROSS

Geneva, Switzerland, is home to the International Committee of the Red Cross (ICRC). Jean-Henri Dunant, a Swiss man, witnessed thousands of soldiers left to die following the Battle of Solferino in 1859. Dunant coordinated care for them, which included help from other civilians. He wrote about the experience in 1862 and received a resounding response. In turn, he formed the International Committee for the Relief of Wounded in 1863, which became the ICRC in 1875. The ICRC established seven fundamental principles: humanity, impartiality, neutrality, independence, voluntary service, unity, and universality. The internationally recognized emblem of the Red Cross is the reverse of the Swiss flag: a red equilateral cross on a white background.

industry and creating new jobs. The banking and insurance industries grew as well.

THE TWENTIETH CENTURY

Switzerland's industry and economy continued to expand as the twentieth century began. When World War I (1914–1918) erupted, Switzerland managed to maintain its neutrality, but the country suffered greatly, partially because of differences between German speakers and the rest of the country. The Swiss society and economy suffered, leading to a brief labor strike and political reforms. In 1919, Switzerland joined the League of Nations, an organization of international cooperation established at the end of World War I.

In the 1930s, impacted by the global depression, Switzerland's exports declined greatly and unemployment increased. Production industries, such as agriculture and textiles, shrank in size. The economy was shifting toward a service industry, meaning that workers provided services such as health, hotels, and finance rather than producing goods.

A second world war broke out in 1939. World War II (1939–1945) was the largest and deadliest war in history, resulting in 40 to 50 million deaths.[4] As Adolf Hitler's Nazi Germany sought to control Europe, Switzerland strove to maintain its neutrality and independence, firmly defending itself after the Nazis overran France in 1940 by creating extensive Alpine defenses.

With limited farmland and natural resources, trading was essential to Switzerland's survival. As a neutral state, Switzerland was allowed to trade with anyone during the war. It traded with both Germany and the United States, and both sides were aware of the situation. From 1940 to 1942, Germany and its ally Italy purchased 45 percent of Swiss exports, which included machinery, iron, tools, chemicals, and vehicles.[5] Switzerland supplied the Nazis with goods that would help them during the war. The Swiss imported goods from the Germans as well, including food and fuel. Swiss banks continued to do business with nations fighting each other in the war, purchasing gold from both sides.

This cooperation with both sides was controversial. Also controversial was the number of refugees flooding the country, especially since the economy was hurting. Many Swiss citizens helped Jews who were being persecuted by the Nazis. But not all Jews were welcomed. Thousands were turned away, some of whom were given over to the Germans.

Switzerland rebounded after the war as imports and exports increased. Industry dominated the economy until services became the primary economic force after approximately 1970. Despite a brief downturn in the 1970s, the postwar period was a time of remarkable growth and prosperity. It was also a time of social and political harmony. Though Swiss voters overwhelmingly rejected membership in the United Nations (UN) in 1986, the country developed a successful

Switzerland guarded its borders during World War II but remained neutral.

SWISS BANKS

The policy of banking secrecy officially began to apply to Swiss banks after the passage of a 1935 law. Banking secrecy means that banks are not allowed to disclose information about clients or accounts to authorities except under very specific circumstances, such as in criminal investigations.

The 1990s brought to light an important banking issue that began threatening this policy. Investigations by multiple countries, including Switzerland itself, revealed thousands of dormant accounts containing millions of dollars belonging to Holocaust victims. This had previously been hidden due to banking secrecy. On August 12, 1998, Swiss banks agreed to repay more than $1.25 billion to Holocaust survivors.[7]

In June 2010, the Swiss parliament approved a plan to give the US Internal Revenue Service (IRS) the names of 4,450 US clients with accounts at UBS, a major Swiss bank.[8] The IRS wanted to prosecute tax evaders. The incident launched arguments about the long-held practice of secrecy by Swiss banks. Swiss President and Finance Minister Eveline Widmer-Schlumpf explained, "Nobody in this chamber wants to remove banking secrecy and that is not the subject of the debate today, we are talking about tax secrets."[9] The issue continues to be debated.

role as an international mediator. The growth slowed after 1989, when Switzerland experienced a severe economic depression and its internal politics became more divided and difficult.

TWENTY-FIRST CENTURY

Switzerland made a rare commitment to international cooperation in the early twenty-first century, finally joining the United Nations in 2002. The international banking crisis brought new challenges in 2008. Economies worldwide suffered, including the historically prosperous Swiss. Swiss banks responded by offering interest-free loans, and the economy rebounded with 2.7 percent growth in 2010.[6]

Following the first decade of the twenty-first century, Switzerland was not faced with the level of political, economic, and social conflict that impacted many countries. Yet the nation faced challenges moving forward. The unique isolationist position of Switzerland united people of different ethnic and linguistic backgrounds, but experts questioned whether this uniqueness could be maintained in a modern environment of globalization, which had brought so many immigrants to Switzerland.

A Swiss representative, *left*, presents a formal request to UN Secretary-General Kofi Annan to join the UN in 2002.

CHAPTER 5

PEOPLE: DIVERSE CULTURES COEXIST

Switzerland's location has made it a crossroads for many European peoples. The nation's four official languages reflect its diversity. Groups that settled certain cantons continue to define them today. Switzerland is also home to thousands of foreigners, totaling almost 23 percent of the resident population as of June 2012.[1]

OFFICIAL LANGUAGES

Switzerland has four official languages: German, French, Italian, and Romansh. They vary greatly in the number of speakers. German is spoken by 63.7 percent of the population.[2] Swiss German is very different from High German, the standard version of the language. The Swiss variation has several dialects that vary by locale. High German is still

Switzerland is home to a wide variety of people and cultures.

MULTILINGUAL

Many Swiss are bilingual, often out of necessity, and children in Swiss schools are taught multiple languages, including English. The Romansh-speaking region is surrounded by the German-speaking region, so the approximately 35,000 Swiss who speak Romansh also speak German.[6] Many Italian speakers also speak German to better compete with the German-speaking region, which dominates the nation in population and economic strength.

used in Switzerland, though primarily in its written form. It is also taught in some schools and is used in the media, including newspapers, magazines, and most books. People familiar solely with High German tend to struggle with Swiss German—its grammar, vocabulary, and accent are all different.

French is spoken by 20.4 percent of Swiss.[3] French is spoken primarily in an area known as the Suisse Romande, in western Switzerland. There are four French-speaking cantons. Three other cantons are bilingual, speaking both French and German.

Italian is spoken by 6.5 percent of Swiss.[4] Italian is the language of the Ticino canton, in southern Switzerland. Italian is also spoken in parts of Graubünden, Ticino's neighbor to the east. Both cantons border Italy.

Romansh is spoken by 0.5 percent of Swiss.[5] The Rhaetians who settled in western Switzerland spoke Romansh. Like other Romance languages, such as French and Italian, it is derived from Latin. Romansh

YOU SAY IT!

English	Swiss German	French	Italian
Hi	Grüezi (GROO-tzee)	Salut (sah-LOO)	Ciao (CHOW)
Good-bye	Auf wiedersehen (owf VEE-der-zay-hen)	Au revoir (oh ruh-VWAR)	Arrivederci (a-ree-vah-DEHR-chee)
Good evening	Guten Abend (goo-ten AH-bend)	Bon soir (bon SWAR)	Buona sera (bwohn-nah SEH-rah)
Thank you	Danke (DONK-uh)	Merci (mer-SEE)	Grazie (GRAHT-tsyeh)

is spoken in the trilingual canton of Graubünden, along with Italian and German.

Several other languages are spoken in Switzerland. Serbo-Croatian is spoken by 1.5 percent of the population; Albanian by 1.3 percent, Portuguese by 1.2 percent, Spanish by 1.1 percent, English by 1 percent, and other unspecified languages by 2.8 percent.[7]

DEMOGRAPHICS

The bulk of Switzerland's approximately 8 million inhabitants belong to one of the ethnic groups that settled the region and speak the nation's official languages. Sixty-five percent of Swiss are German, 18 percent are French, 10 percent are Italian, and 1 percent are Romansh. The remaining 6 percent belong to other minority ethnic groups.[8]

Most Swiss—67.8 percent—are between the ages of 15 and 54. Seventeen percent of the population is 65 years or older, while 15.2 percent of Swiss are 14 years or younger.[9] The average life expectancy is 81.17 years, which makes Switzerland seventeenth in the world for life expectancy. The average life expectancy for Swiss males and females is 78.34 years and 84.16 years, respectively.[10]

The 2012 estimates for death and birth rates are 8.8 and 9.51 per 1,000 Swiss,

FAMILY STATISTICS

In Switzerland, men and women marry relatively late. The average age at first marriage is 28.7 for women and 31 for men. Swiss women also tend to have their first child relatively late: 29.5 is their average age. Swiss women also bear fewer children than the world average. Most Swiss families have one or two children.[11] Couples limit family size primarily because of finances.

Switzerland's ethnic diversity means there is a wide variety of festivals and celebrations.

MOST POPULAR NAMES

Each year, Switzerland publishes the most popular baby names. In 2010, the most popular names for boys and girls were Noah and Lena (German), Nathan and Emma (French), and Mattia and Guilia (Italian).

respectively. Due to an immigration rate of 1.27 people per 1,000 Swiss, the population is still growing at an estimated rate of 0.199 percent annually. Swiss women give birth to an average of 1.47 children.[12]

Most of Switzerland's inhabitants—74 percent— live in cities.[13] The remaining 26 percent live in rural areas, including in the mountains. Zurich has the highest population of all Swiss cities: 1.143 million people. Bern, the nation's capital, is home to 346,000 people.[14]

RELIGIONS

Switzerland does not have an official religion, though many cantons recognize official churches. The Christian religions that shaped Switzerland's history remain prevalent: 41.8 percent of Swiss people are Roman Catholic, and 35.3 percent are Protestant.[15] However, the importance of religion has declined, as has the frequency of going to church: 38.5 percent of Catholics do not attend church. The figure is higher for Protestants: 50.7 percent do not attend church.[16] Church events such as weddings, baptisms, and funerals have declined dramatically

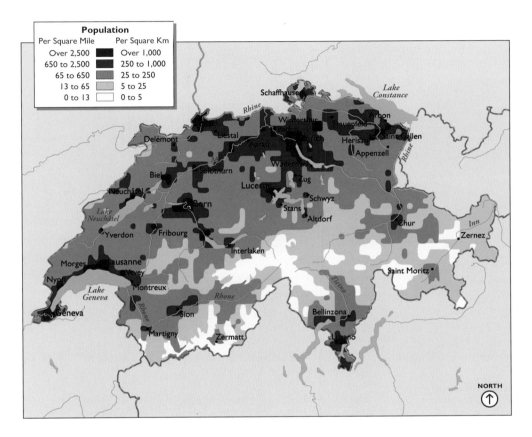

Population Density of Switzerland

Swiss voters banned the construction of minarets in 2009.

over the last 30 years. Slightly more than one in ten Swiss do not claim a religious affiliation, while 4.3 percent do not specify a religion. Eastern Orthodox and other forms of Christianity are followed by 2.2 percent of the population. The number of Swiss practicing Judaism, Hinduism, and Buddhism totals less than 1 percent combined.[17]

Islam is on the rise in Switzerland and has the next highest number of followers after Catholicism and Protestantism. Muslims account for 4.3 percent of the Swiss population.[18] Swiss Muslims are predominantly Balkan and Turkish. The percentage of Muslims almost doubled between 1990 and 2000.[19] The growth of this population troubles some Swiss. In 2009, citizens voted to ban minarets, towers which are a part of the mosques where Muslims worship.

MINARETS PROHIBITED

In November 2009, a majority of Swiss voters approved a proposed ban on the construction of minarets. These towers are a feature of mosque architecture. The proposed ban was put forward by the Swiss People's Party, which argued that minarets—of which there were four in the country, none of which played the traditional call to prayer—symbolize Islam, a religion many terrorists have claimed to follow. The party claimed the building of minarets implied that Switzerland is becoming an Islamic nation.

The government was against the ban, fearing that it would negatively affect the Swiss image, but it accepted the vote. The government issued a statement: "The Federal Council (government) respects this decision. Consequently the construction of new minarets in Switzerland is no longer permitted."[20]

CHAPTER 6
CULTURE: UNITED, NOT UNIFORM

The Swiss are expert cheese makers and have been making cheese for thousands of years. Gruyère and Emmentaler are just two of the many varieties available. Switzerland is also known for fondue, a mixture of melted cheeses and wine into which bread is dipped.

Swiss cuisine varies by region. Popular alpine dishes include: raclette, or bread or potatoes topped with cheese melted over a fire; *rösti*, or hash browns; *älpler magrone*, or macaroni and cheese served with bacon, onions, and cinnamon applesauce; and *birchermüsli, or* oats, nuts, and fruit with yogurt.

More than 450 types of Swiss cheese are officially recognized.

Switzerland is well known for its wide variety of cheeses.

Dishes with dumplings, pasta, or potatoes are popular in the central and southern valleys. Spaetzle (small dumplings) and *knöpfli* (small noodles) serve as both a side dish and as part of a main dish. People in areas near Austria and Germany often eat meat dishes from those neighboring countries, such as *weisswurst* (white veal sausage), *leberknodli* (liver dumplings), and *schublig* (sausages baked in bread). French areas such as Geneva enjoy French cuisine, while Italian cooking influences southern areas. Several regions enjoy soup, and fish is popular.

In 2011, the Swiss chocolate industry sold almost 389 million pounds (176 million kg) of chocolate.

Swiss cuisine includes sweets. The Swiss are famous for their chocolate. Other desserts include: *lebkuchen*, or spiced Christmas cookies made with molasses and candied fruit; *leckerli*, or spiced honey cakes; *tarte aux poivres*, or pear flan; and *zugerkirschtorte*, or cherry brandy tart.

The Swiss also enjoy alcoholic beverages. The popularity of Swiss wine, combined with its limited production, leaves little for export. Beers are particularly popular in the German regions, and a variety of spirits are consumed. The Swiss make liqueurs from a selection of fruits, including cherry pits, grape skins, pears, plums, and prunes.

MUSIC

Folk music is performed mostly in rural areas. Yodeling, a traditional form of singing, and the alpenhorn are associated with Switzerland, though they

are not exclusive to the Swiss. Yodeling is believed to have begun during the Stone Age, when yodeling was used to call cows and to communicate across distances.

DANCE IN SWITZERLAND

Alpine culture includes traditional dances such as the Ländler, which is waltz-like, and the Schuhplattler, which involves jumping and hopping quickly. Béjart Ballet Lausanne, the national ballet company, was founded in 1987. Switzerland also has numerous professional dance companies, many of them specializing in modern and contemporary styles.

The alpenhorn is an alpine instrument. This horn is very long, extending several feet from the player's mouth with its base resting on the ground. It is made of wood and bark. Other traditional instruments include the *Schwyzerörgeli*, a type of accordion, and the *hackbrett*, an instrument with strings stretched over a trapezoidal sounding board.

Swiss music was primarily for religious purposes until the seventeenth century. Music became livelier in the nineteenth century, when choral music became popular. Internationally known Swiss composers from the twentieth century include Arthur Honegger, Frank Martin, and Othmar Schoeck. Today, several Swiss cities have orchestras. Pop and rock songs are frequently sung in English, though several Swiss performers sing in their own dialect. This style is known as Mundartrock, or "dialect rock."

Two major music events take place every summer. The Lucerne Festival, which features classical music, is held in August. The Montreux

Jazz Festival attracts jazz lovers from around the world to the town of Montreux in southwest Switzerland.

HOLIDAYS AND FESTIVALS

Switzerland celebrates several national holidays: New Year's Day, Good Friday, Easter, Easter Monday, Ascension Day, Whit Sunday and Monday, National Day (August 1), Christmas Day, and Boxing Day.

In addition, several cantons celebrate particular days as local holidays. January 2 is Bechtold's Day in 14 cantons, in honor of the founder of Bern. Six cantons honor January 6 as Epiphany, or Three Kings Day, the Christian celebration of three wise men meeting the baby Jesus.

The Swiss have many festivals. In Zurich, Sechseläuten marks the beginning of spring. The April festival includes parades, traditional costumes, and a burning of the Böögg, a snowman-shaped figure filled with firecrackers. Chästeilet highlights the end of the summer alpine season. Cheese made that

TRADITIONAL SWISS COSTUMES

Though traditional Swiss costumes differ from region to region, there are many common elements. Women's costumes often feature puffy blouses, floral embroidery, and red or white tights. Men's costumes tend to include loose-fitting shirts and trousers. Men from Switzerland's alpine regions wear lederhosen, or leather shorts with suspenders.

season is split between the owners of the cows whose milk was used in the cheese production. Usually held in September, the holiday features cows with flowers in their horns. Autumn festivals showcase crops and include chestnut fairs, the onion market in Bern, and a three-day festival in Neuchâtel. Trychle occurs the last week of December, between Christmas and New Year's Day. Participants wear disguises and make noise with cowbells and drums. The Swiss mark the beginning of Lent with Fasnacht. Similar to Carnival or Mardi Gras, the celebrations vary and usually involve costumes and music. Basel's celebration is popular.

FOLKLORE

Two figures stand out among Switzerland's varied folklore. The Barbegazi are timid little men with white fur and long frozen beards. They live in the mountains and ski to town on their giant feet. Jack o' the Bowl lives indoors, keeping watch over people in return for a nightly bowl of cream.

SPORTS

The Swiss enjoy a variety of sports, with winter sports being particularly popular. Switzerland has many ski resorts and trails for cross-country

Sechseläuten is a festival celebrating the return of spring.

skiing. Curling is another favorite winter sport. Saint Moritz hosted the Winter Olympics in 1928 and 1948.

Switzerland's many lakes offer opportunities for sailing, swimming, and paragliding. Other sports enjoyed by the Swiss include shooting, soccer, tennis, golf, hockey, basketball, handball, and gliding. Among the most popular is *schwingen*, a traditional form of wrestling that has survived for centuries. Competitors must pin an opponent's shoulder blades to the ground while maintaining a hold on his belt. Cycling is also popular, and several major races take place in Switzerland, including the Tour de Suisse and the Tour de Romandie. Currently, Fabian Cancellera is among the most successful Swiss cyclists. He won gold and silver medals at the 2008 Summer Olympics, and placed first in the Tour de Suisse in 2009.

Roger Federer has won four Australian Opens, one French Open, seven Wimbledons, and five US Opens.

Roger Federer is Switzerland's best known and most successful athlete. He dominated men's professional tennis in the early twenty-first century and was ranked the top male tennis player in the world for a record 237 consecutive weeks.[1] In 2009, he broke the record for the most major tennis tournaments won.

Like many nations around the globe, Switzerland has a strong love of soccer. The Swiss Football

The mountains of Switzerland make for excellent ski areas.

Association was founded in 1895 and includes 12,887 teams and approximately 231,000 players across all levels of play.[2]

WILLIAM TELL

William Tell is a mythical Swiss hero. According to the legend, in the fourteenth century he defied authority by refusing to bow to a hat placed on a pole by Gessler, an imperial official. Gessler arrested Tell for treason and threatened to execute him unless Tell could shoot an apple off his own son's head. Tell succeeded, explaining later that he had a second arrow and would have killed Gessler if his son had been injured.

The official arrested Tell anyway and put him on a boat to be sent to a prison. A storm came up. Tell convinced his captors to unchain him so he could navigate the craft through waters that he alone was familiar with. Instead, he jumped overboard after sending the boat into rough waters. Once ashore, Tell found Gessler, shot him through the heart with his last arrow, and vanished. The story was given great prominence by the German dramatist Friedrich Schiller in 1804 and the Italian composer Giaochino Rossini 25 years later.

LITERATURE

Achieving fame and wealth as a writer in Switzerland is challenging. The population is relatively small, which limits the audience. The number of official languages further limits purchasers for any single book. Switzerland does have a publishing industry that produces thousands of books annually, but most famous Swiss writers are from centuries past.

Jean-Jacques Rousseau wrote about philosophy and politics in such works as *Discourse on the Origin of Inequality* (1755) and *The Social Contract* (1762). Johann Rudolf

Wyss completed and edited *The Swiss Family Robinson* (1812–1827), a novel begun by his father. Johanna Spyri penned *Heidi* (1880–1881), the beloved children's book. Poet Carl Spitteler received the Nobel Prize for Literature in 1919; Herman Hesse, author of *Siddhartha* (1922), was awarded the prize in 1946. The notable modernist writer Robert Walser was largely forgotten by the time of his death in 1956, but his work was rediscovered, translated, and widely reprinted in the 1970s.

FILM AND THEATER

The Swiss film industry is small, and its films are not generally known internationally, with the exception of those by Jean-Luc Godard and Alain Tanner. In 1991, *Journey of Hope* won an Oscar for best foreign film. Locarno, located in southern Switzerland, hosts an international film festival each year.

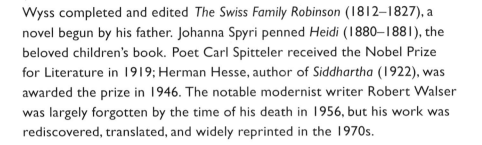

The Locarno film festival features a huge open-air screening area that seats more than 8,000.

Swiss theater has often highlighted religious themes. Patriotic plays developed in the nineteenth century. This prompted the construction of municipal theaters throughout Switzerland. Today, plays in French-speaking regions are often performed in settings other than theaters, such as schools. Independent theater groups perform in towns without theaters in Italian and Romansh regions.

Two notable playwrights emerged in the wake of World War II, and their works were deeply influenced by it. Friedrich Durrenmatt

In Friedrich Durrenmatt's twist-filled *Die Physiker*, two men apparently believe themselves to be Albert Einstein and Isaac Newton.

used satire in his writing, perhaps most notably in his 1962 play *Die Physiker* (The Physicists). Max Frisch wrote novels as well as plays, and notably used irony in his works. Durrenmatt and Frisch died in 1990 and 1991, respectively.

ARCHITECTURE

Swiss architecture reflects a variety of styles. Cathedrals and churches in many cities feature Romanesque, Gothic, and Baroque design. Houses in eastern Switzerland are often made of lath and plaster, a practice that began in the fifteenth century and was prominent in the eighteenth century. In the south, Ticino houses tend to be small and made of stone, while the Mittelland region has combination homes that include a barn. The iconic chalet is plentiful. Made of wood but often with a stone base, it has an A-frame roof and is adorned with colorful window shutters and window boxes of flowers.

Le Corbusier was an important architect of the twentieth century. Born in Switzerland in 1887 as Charles-Édouard Jeanneret, Le Corbusier designed towns and furniture in addition to buildings. He is known for suggesting modern principles for architecture in 1923: rationality, economy, and functionalism.

Mario Botta has designed buildings in Switzerland and other countries, including banks, churches, and museums. The works of Jacques Herzog and Pierre de Meuron include the famous Tate Modern museum in

HELVETICA

The typeface Helvetica was created in 1957 by Max Miedinger, a Swiss graphic designer and typographer. The typeface was initially called Neue Hass-Grotesk. In 1960, Miedinger changed the name to Helvetica, after his homeland. Helvetica is a popular font around the world. Major companies have used it in their branding, including Gap, Hoover, Panasonic, Toyota, and Tupperware. Due to its readability, Helvetica is also popular for street signs.

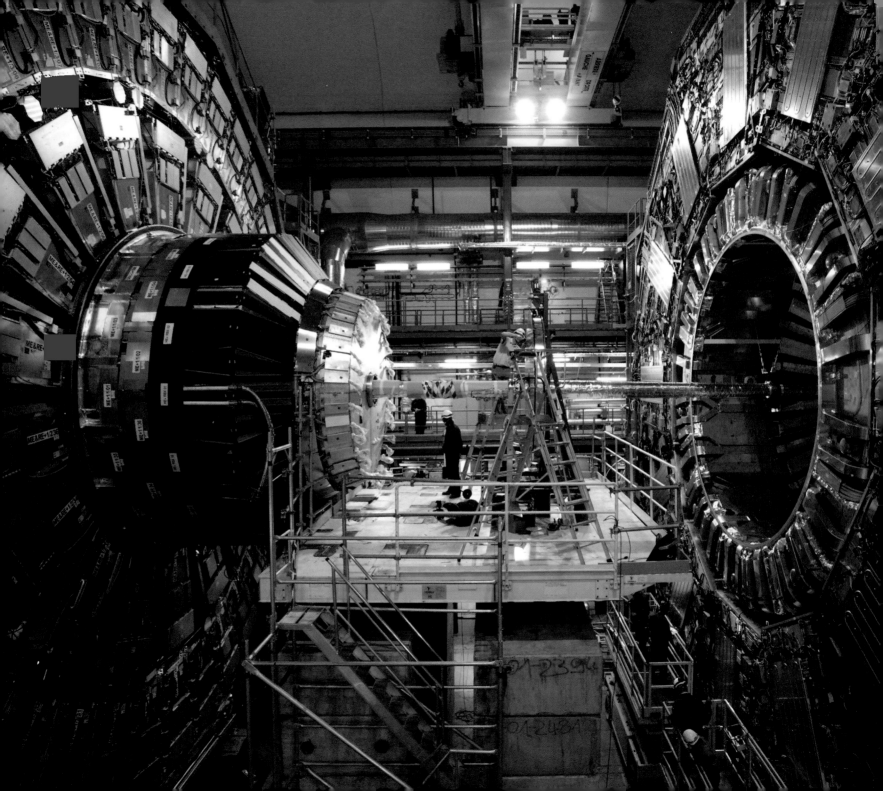

London and the Beijing National Stadium, known as "the Bird's Nest" during the 2008 Summer Olympics.

SCIENCE

Switzerland has been home to scientists from many fields. Paracelsus introduced chemistry to medicine in the early sixteenth century, and Daniel Bernoulli contributed significantly to mathematics and the sciences during the mid-1700s. Jean Piaget and Carl Jung were highly influential psychologists in the twentieth century. Several Nobel Prize winners in physics worked at Zurich's Federal Institute of Technology, including Albert Einstein (1921), Wolfgang Pauli (1945), and Heinrich Rohrer (1986).

Switzerland is home to the Large Hadron Collider (LHC), the largest and most powerful particle accelerator in the world. It allows scientists to conduct high-energy physics experiments. The LHC's circular tunnel is located on the border with France 165 to 575 feet (50 to 175 m) underground. It is 17 miles (27 km) long.[3] On July 4, 2012, scientists working at the LHC announced findings that were consistent with the discovery of the Higgs boson. The Higgs boson is a hypothetical subatomic particle that is responsible for giving objects mass. The scientists cautioned that more work needed to be done to be certain about their findings, but the announcement was seen as a significant breakthrough in particle physics.

Costing nearly US$5 billion, the Large Hadron Collider is one of the most expensive scientific instruments in history.

CHAPTER 7

POLITICS: SWISS DEMOCRACY

The 1848 Swiss constitution established the political system in place today. Modifications have since strengthened the direct democratic element, which has deep roots in Swiss history. Swiss voters now play a tremendous part in the political process, giving their direct input on issues that affect them and their country.

THE SWISS FLAG

The Swiss flag is a red square containing a white cross with arms of equal length. Military forces of the Swiss Confederation began wearing white crosses on their uniforms as early as 1339, but the basic design was not adopted as the Swiss flag until 1848. In 1889 a slight change was made to the dimensions of the cross, and the flag has remained the same since then. The Swiss flag is one of only two square national flags in the world. The other is used by Vatican City.

Switzerland's national flag

Switzerland is one of the oldest of the world's federal states, countries that include self-governing regions and a central government. The Swiss modeled their original national constitution after the US Constitution. The constitution was revised in 1874 to include the right to referendum, giving the Swiss people the ability to challenge bills passed in Parliament. Another revision in 1891 added the popular initiative, allowing voters to propose new amendments to the Constitution. In the cantons there is an even larger array of direct democratic methods. In 1999 voters approved a completely revised constitution that went into effect in 2000. The new document made constitutional law more easily understandable, updating the language and terminology to make it fit with modern standards of law and rights.

LEVELS OF GOVERNMENT

Switzerland has three levels of government: communes, cantons, and federal. Communes are the smallest pieces of government. Communal responsibilities include keeping basic records and overseeing local planning, schools, and taxes. In approximately 80 percent of communes, citizens vote on issues directly.[1] The remaining communes have elected representatives who vote on behalf of the citizens. Communes vary in their level of autonomy, which is decided by the cantons.

The Federal Palace in Bern

STRUCTURE OF THE GOVERNMENT OF SWITZERLAND

Executive Branch	Legislative Branch	Judicial Branch
Federal Council	National Council Council of States	Federal Supreme Court

The federal government is the highest level of government. Switzerland's federal government has three branches: legislative, judicial, and executive.

LEGISLATIVE BRANCH

The Federal Assembly, or parliament, is the legislative branch. It is bicameral, meaning there are two separate legislative bodies. The first, called the National Council, has 200 members. Elections are held using a proportional representation system. Citizens vote for parties, and the proportion of votes each party gets will be the proportion of National Council seats they receive. The second, called the Council of States, has 46 members who represent the cantons: 20 cantons have two members each, while the six half cantons have one member. Each canton elects its own members to send to the Council, using any kind of democratic election process it chooses. The two chambers have exactly the same powers.

The Swiss cast their votes for the National Council and Council of States every four years; there are no term limits. Swiss citizens may vote and run for office at age 18. The Federal Assembly passes federal laws, approves the national budget, and helps determine foreign policy. It also elects the members of the judicial and executive branches.

POLITICAL PARTIES

Several political parties are active in Switzerland. Generally, the four biggest parties make up the federal government. The top four parties in 2012 were the Swiss People's Party, the Swiss Social Democratic Party, the FDP Liberals, and the Christian Democrat People's Party. Seven more political parties were represented in Swiss parliament in 2012: the Swiss Green Party, the Swiss Green Liberal Party, the Conservative Democratic Party, the Evangelical People's Party, the Ticino League, the Christian Social Party Obwalden, and the Geneva Citizens' Movement.

JUDICIAL BRANCH

Switzerland's judiciary has four courts: the Federal Supreme Court and the three federal courts of first instance, which are the Federal Criminal Court, the Federal Administrative Court, and the Federal Patent Court. The Federal Supreme Court hears appeals to decisions of the first instance courts and some cantonal courts.

The federal judiciary has 38 full-time judges and 19 part-time judges.[2] Each judge is chosen by the Federal Assembly to serve a six-year term. The Federal Assembly also selects from this group a president and vice president of the court. Each serves a two-year term. The president of the Federal Supreme Court oversees the court and represents the court to the public.

EXECUTIVE BRANCH

The executive branch is led by the Federal Council, a government with seven members elected by the Federal Assembly every four years. In 2012, they represented five separate political parties. The Federal Council operates seven ministries, or departments: finance; foreign affairs; economic affairs; home affairs; justice and police; defense, civil protection, and sport; and environment, transport, energy, and communications. Each member heads one ministry.

The president of Switzerland, one of the federal councillors, is elected to a one-year term by the Federal Assembly. The council member serving as president is considered *prima inter pares*, or "first among equals." While acting as president, the council member manages Federal Council meetings and takes on ceremonial duties in addition to overseeing his or her ministry. In 2012, the president was Eveline Widmer-Schlumpf, who was also the finance minister.

Eveline Widmer-Schlumpf was the sixth woman ever elected to the Federal Council.

Members of parliament work during a session of the Federal Assembly in 2011.

Per the constitution, all members of the Federal Council are equal. They meet weekly, voting on proposals brought to them by the seven departments. The council makes decisions in private and then presents them to the public unanimously—all members support the decision, even when not in the majority.

The Federal Assembly also elects the federal chancellor. The federal chancellor is supported by two vice chancellors and 250 staffers. The Federal Chancellery oversees the electoral process. It also prepares agendas for the weekly Federal Council meetings. Each meeting averages 100 agenda items.[3] The federal chancellor may speak in Federal Council meetings and propose motions, but he or she may not vote.

WOMEN AND FEDERAL ELECTIONS

This history of Swiss women's participation in federal elections has been relatively short. After a failed attempt in 1959, women were granted the right to participate and vote in federal elections in 1971. Elisabeth Kopp became the first woman in Swiss government when she was elected to the Federal Council in 1984. In 2010, women outnumbered men in the Federal Council for the first time in the nation's history.

POPULAR INITIATIVES AND REFERENDUMS

In Switzerland, voting is more important than electing. The Federal Assembly has less power than federal legislatures in other countries, and less power than the people. Swiss voters make decisions directly. They are the final political authority.

Swiss voters also decide on federal proposals. Generally, federal proposals are voted on up to four times a year, with three or four

proposals up for a vote each time. Voters decide on popular initiatives, items proposed by a person or group of people, not the legislative or executive branch. In order to be eligible for a vote, 100,000 signatures of voters who support the initiative must be obtained within 18 months.[4]

There are two types of referendums. A mandatory referendum concerns a constitutional amendment or a proposal to join an international organization. A mandatory referendum is automatically put on the ballot for popular vote. An optional referendum involves a challenge to a federal law, a parliamentary decision, or an international treaty. To be put on the ballot, an optional referendum must obtain 50,000 signatures from supporting voters within 100 days.[5]

Voter turnout for federal votes—those for initiatives and referendums—averages less than 50 percent.[6] However, turnout varies depending on the subject of the initiative or referendum. In 1989, 69 percent of voters voted on an initiative to get rid of the nation's army.[7] The initiative was not approved.

A man exits a Swiss voting booth during the 2007 election.

CHAPTER 8
ECONOMICS: SERVICE FOCUSED

Switzerland is a prosperous nation. While it has few natural resources, it has a highly developed service industry, a strong manufacturing sector, and productive agriculture. These characteristics have resulted in strong trading partnerships that total approximately $300 billion each in imports and exports.[1] The Swiss economy also benefits from its highly developed infrastructure, its high educational levels, and low unemployment.

Switzerland's total production in 2011 was US$691.5 billion

NATURAL RESOURCES

Switzerland's limited natural resources include salt, timber, and hydropower. Salt is the nation's only product that comes

Key among Switzerland's few natural resources is its hydropower capacity.

from mines. Though Switzerland possesses abundant forests, the nation has strict restrictions on cutting because of the importance of trees to the environment. As a result, Switzerland tends to import more timber than it exports.

Switzerland relies heavily on its water sources for power. The nation has an extensive network of dams and reservoirs, as well as rivers, where running water drives power station turbines.

A STRONG SERVICE INDUSTRY

People are perhaps Switzerland's greatest resource, thanks to their high level of education and their strength in research and development. Their work in the service industry is the backbone of the Swiss economy. The service segment accounts for 71.3 percent of Switzerland's gross domestic product (GDP), the total output of the country divided by the total population. The service industry also employs 73.2 percent of the labor force.[2] The primary service industries are banking, tourism, and insurance.

Switzerland is known for banking. This segment of Swiss economy had 195,000 employees in 2009, comprising 5.8 percent of the nation's workforce. Credit Suisse and UBS control more than 30 percent of the domestic industry, with assets approximately six times greater than the nation's GDP.[3] Switzerland is also a leader in the insurance industry.

Switzerland's scenic landscapes are popular destinations for tourists.

Swiss insurance companies service the Swiss as well as others, with half of their earnings coming from abroad.

Tourism is another important sector of the Swiss economy. In 2008, foreign tourists accounted for 3 percent of the GDP.[4] The greatest portion of them came from Germany, followed by the United States, Great Britain, and Japan. The Swiss tour their own country as well.

Travel increased dramatically in the latter half of the twentieth century. The most popular destination is the Alps, accounting for the majority of overnight visits. The millions of visitors who stay in hotels, guesthouses, campsites, and other locations are serviced by thousands of workers. In 2005, 4.4 percent of Swiss workers were in the tourism industry.[5]

NESTLÉ

Switzerland's largest company is the world's largest food company: Nestlé. In 2009, the food giant had approximately 278,000 employees, nearly all of whom worked outside Switzerland.[7] Nestlé makes a variety of products under numerous brands, including Gerber baby food; Perrier bottled water; Butterfinger, Crunch, and Kit Kat candy bars; Lean Cuisine and Stouffer's frozen foods; Carnation dairy products; Nestea iced tea; Häagen Dazs ice cream; and Purina pet food. The company also owns Jenny Craig, a popular weight management program in the United States.

MANUFACTURING

The industrial sector, including manufacturing, accounts for 27.5 percent of the GDP and employs 23.4 percent of Swiss workers, many of whom are highly skilled.[6] The sector includes such products as watches,

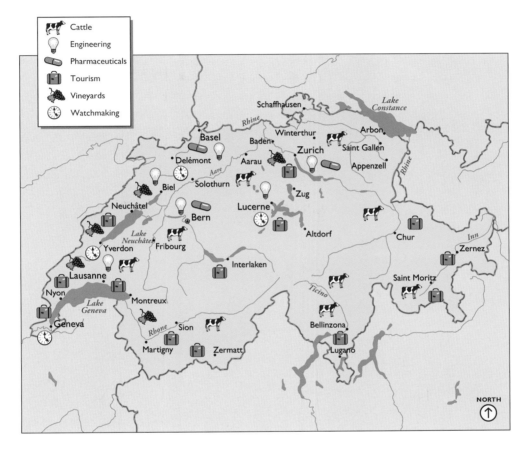

Resources of Switzerland

chemicals, and pharmaceuticals, as well as mechanical and electrical engineering. Switzerland is at the forefront of the pharmaceuticals and chemical industry. It is home to pharmaceutical giants Novartis and Roche. Chemicals produced include dyes, flavorings, and perfumes.

Mechanical and electrical engineering make up a key sector of the economy. They include four distinct areas: electrical engineering and electronics, mechanical engineering and vehicle construction, metallurgy, and precision instruments. Most of the goods built in Switzerland, including household items, machine tools, and microelectronic equipment, are exported. Overall, Switzerland is one of the world's most innovative and competitive countries.

Watchmaking is a Swiss specialty. The Swiss are known for their quality timepieces, which include the brands Rolex and Omega, as well as the popular Swatch. Switzerland exports most of the timepieces it creates.

AGRICULTURE

Agriculture accounts for 1.3 percent of Switzerland's GDP and employs 3.4 percent of Swiss workers.[8] Approximately one-third of Swiss land is used for agriculture.[9] Since 1990, the number of farms has decreased by almost half, but the average size of a farm has nearly

Watchmaking is a major Swiss industry.

doubled.[10] Switzerland's major agricultural products include eggs, fruit, vegetables, grains, and meat.

Cattle make up the largest portion of Swiss livestock. In 2010, Switzerland's cattle population was 1,591,233. Of this, 700,315 animals were cows.[11] This segment of the industry includes dairy farming, which produces milk, butter, cheese, and yogurt.

INFRASTRUCTURE

Switzerland has a multifaceted and well-coordinated transportation system that links the major cities and allows access to all regions. The Swiss are avid train riders, thanks in part to an efficient and helpful ticketing system. The government operates Swiss Federal Railways, which owns more than 50 percent of the nation's rail system. The rail line has a network of 1,965 miles (3,163 km) and continues to expand. Private railroad companies operate an additional 1,250 miles (2,000 km) of track.[12] Hundreds of tunnels and passes allow access through rugged mountains, and bridges span gorges.

Trains also allow for easy transport to the major airports near Zurich and Geneva. Kloten, located near Zurich, is the nation's main airport. Geneva and Basel have major airports as well. Bern and Lugano have smaller airports, and many more small airports are located

Trains make traveling across Switzerland easy and efficient.

THE SWISS FRANC

Switzerland's currency is the Swiss franc. One hundred centimes equal one franc, just as 100 pennies equal one dollar. Bills are available in values of 10, 20, 50, 100, 200, and 1,000 francs. They feature portraits of Swiss artists and include printed information in all four Swiss languages. Coins are minted in values of 5, 10, 20, and 50 centimes as well as 1, 2, and 5 francs. Different coins include images of Libertas, the Roman goddess of liberty, Helvetia, a female figure symbolic of Switzerland, and an alpine herdsman.

throughout the country. Swiss International Airlines, the national airline, is now owned by the German carrier Lufthansa.

Driving is popular in Switzerland, and car ownership is on the rise. In 2006, almost 52 percent of Swiss owned cars.[13] This is among the highest automobile ownership rates in Europe. In 2009, Switzerland had 1,112 miles (1,789 km) of roads.[14] Not all car drivers are car owners. Companies sell shared car subscriptions to customers throughout Switzerland.

Switzerland relies on a variety of energy sources. Hydroelectricity figures prominently, providing more than half of the nation's energy production.[15] Nuclear energy ranks second. Switzerland has four nuclear power plants, but after the 2011 nuclear disaster in Fukushima, Japan,

Swiss currency

the Swiss have decided to begin phasing them out. Some power stations in Switzerland use thermal power, burning fossil fuels or garbage to boil water. The steam then spins a turbine, creating electricity. Other energy sources include solar power and wind power.

Internet usage in Switzerland increased dramatically between 2000 and 2010, growing from 28.8 percent of the population to 75.3 percent.[16] The Swiss Broadcasting Corporation is the nation's primary provider of television and radio stations. The company has a collection of media outlets, including three German-language television networks and two networks each in Italian and French. In addition, the company offers programming in Romansh. The Swiss Broadcasting Corporation also owns 18 radio stations: six in German, four in French, three in Italian, one in Romansh, one in English, and three that play music.

IMPORTS AND EXPORTS

With few natural resources, Switzerland relies heavily on trade for the materials it needs. Switzerland ranks eighteenth in the world for imports, buying agricultural products, chemicals, machinery, metals, textiles, and vehicles from other countries. Its major import partner is Germany, from which Switzerland obtains 32 percent of its imported goods. Switzerland also trades with Italy (10.2 percent), France (8.6 percent), the United States (5 percent), the Netherlands (4.4 percent), and Austria (4.3 percent). All told, the European Union (EU) supplies approximately 80 percent of Switzerland's imports.[17]

Switzerland exports a variety of commodities, including agricultural products, chemicals, machinery, metals, and watches. Switzerland ranks twentieth in the world for exports, selling primarily to Germany, which buys 20.2 percent of Swiss goods. The United States (10.3 percent), Italy (7.7 percent), France (7.1 percent), and the United Kingdom (4.8 percent) are also partners. Combined, the EU receives approximately 60 percent of Switzerland's exports.[18]

COPING WITH THE EUROPEAN UNION

Switzerland is not a part of the European Union (EU). Swiss voters declined starting immediate membership negotiations in 2001. The Swiss question the benefits of joining the EU, which would require changing the Swiss system of democracy, likely cost the nation financially, and possibly challenge the nation's neutral stance.

INCOME, POVERTY, AND WORKERS

Switzerland is financially successful. Its 2011 estimated unemployment rate was 3.1 percent. This figure was a drop of 0.8 percent from 2010 and ranks the nation as twenty-eighth lowest in the world for unemployment.[19]

Per capita income in Switzerland is also high and improving. This is a measure of all income in the country divided by the total population. It was estimated as US$42,500 in 2009, US$43,400 in 2010, and

US$43,900 in 2011. In 2011, Switzerland had the fifteenth highest per capita income in the world.[20] The poverty rate in 2010 was 6.9 percent.[21]

While its economic situation is improving, Switzerland still faces challenges. With fewer young people and births, the Swiss workforce will begin shrinking. Switzerland's reliance on foreign workers will have to grow to meet the nation's need for employees. In addition, the younger population will become responsible for the growing aging population.

Approximately one-fourth of Swiss workers are members of a trade union.

Switzerland is also facing a new reality: economic growth is not unlimited. The Swiss were not immune to the recessions that developed at the end of the first decade of the twenty-first century. And the country's banking system continues to grapple with issues of secrecy, tax evasion, and tax fraud.

As older Swiss retire, the population slowdown means that it may become difficult to replace them.

CHAPTER 9
SWITZERLAND TODAY

Life in Switzerland is similar to life in the United States. Many adults work, while children, teens, and young adults attend school. Some families have both parents living together, but many others do not: the divorce rate is increasing and was more than 50 percent in 2005. The percentage of working mothers with children ages 15 and younger has increased as well, growing from 61 percent in 1991 to 74 percent in 2001.[1] One key difference between the two countries is that military service is required for many young Swiss.

The Swiss entertain themselves in a variety of ways. Many enjoy playing sports or simply being outdoors. Art and cultural activities are valued, varying from traditional festivals to the fine arts. The Swiss enjoy watching television. They also like to travel, with France, Germany, Italy, and Spain being the top destinations.

Switzerland's high divorce rate, up from just 13 percent in 1970, has created many more single-parent families.

EDUCATION

Switzerland has come to rely on knowledge and skills as resources. As such, education is important. The Swiss education system has multiple levels: preprimary (kindergarten), primary (grades 1 through 6), lower (grades 7 through 9) and upper (grades 10 up to 14) secondary, and tertiary (university or higher vocational education). Most schools are public and overseen by the cantons.

Kindergarten is optional and can range from one to three years, depending on location. Children enter primary school at age six. The primary and lower secondary levels are required and total nine years of schooling. During these years, students study their mother language, one of the other national languages, and English.

SWISS TELEVISION HABITS

Almost 75 percent of Swiss watch television daily. Viewing varies by language. Swiss in Italian-speaking areas average 188 minutes per day, while those in French-speaking regions average 161. Swiss living in the German and Romansh areas have the lowest average, 145 minutes.[2]

Swiss children gather in protest of child labor in the developing world.

HARMONIZATION

In 2006, the Swiss voted to create more consistency in their school systems in a process known as harmonization. Education is overseen primarily at the canton level, which has resulted in great variance. Harmonization will create standards intended to develop consistency in the teaching of science, math, and foreign languages. Students will also be expected to meet learning benchmarks.

While in the lower secondary level, students receive basic general education that varies by school. Some schools prepare students for continued study; others are more practical and prepare students for apprenticeships in which they will train for a profession such as woodworking or watchmaking. Following the lower secondary level, students can either continue their studies or join the workforce. This decision happens much earlier for Swiss children than for American children.

Once students complete the lower secondary level, they have finished their required education. Students moving on to the upper secondary level prepare for the next level of study. At the tertiary level, students attend a university or an advanced technical school. Switzerland has two national polytechnics, ten cantonal public universities, eight applied science colleges, and 15 teacher education colleges.[3]

Swiss students at a secondary school in Basel

Because schools are run by individual cantons, start and stop times vary. Lunch times vary as well, lasting up to two hours. The inconsistencies between schools can be problematic for families with children attending different schools.

CHALLENGES

As the Swiss move further into the twenty-first century, they face a variety of economic and environmental challenges. Each year, more than 3,700 people are estimated to suffer an early death due to the effects of air pollution, which can cause asthma, bronchitis, heart attack, and lung cancer.[4] To combat the problem, railways are being expanded under the Alps. The goal is to get people to drive less and take the train more to decrease air pollution. There is also talk of another Saint Gotthard road tunnel.

Environmental endeavors also involve maintaining species, including those animals that have been introduced. Climate change could increase its threats to Switzerland's unique ecosystems. Hydroelectricity, a valued

RECYCLING

Recycling is a priority in Switzerland. Some cantons tax households by making them pay a fee for every bag of garbage they put out. If a bag does not have a tax stamp, it will not be collected. The more recycling one does, the less garbage is put out for collection, and the less tax one pays. In 2003, the Swiss recycled 95 percent of glass, 85 to 90 percent of aluminum cans, 75 percent of tin cans, 71 percent of plastic, and 70 percent of paper.[5]

Swiss people cherish their spectacular landscapes.

THE SWISS PATH

Switzerland inaugurated a footpath to celebrate its 700th birthday in 1991. The trail is in central Switzerland and begins in Rütli Meadow, the birthplace of Switzerland. The 22-mile (36 km) path circles Lake Uri and ends at the village of Brunnen.[7] Sites include chapels and castles. The path consists of 26 sections, one for each canton. The sections are sized in proportion to the canton's population, and are placed in order of when each became part of the confederation.

renewable resource that helps in the fight against pollution, is creating problems of its own. Hydroelectric plants are taking up valuable land and affecting rivers by modifying water flow.

The agricultural industry also faces challenges. Farming is increasingly becoming the second form of income for farmers. More than two-thirds of Swiss farmers rely on nonagricultural sources for their primary income.[6] Some raise exotic animals such as ostriches and yaks to make additional money, while others offer llama treks.

There are also political challenges, as the Swiss attempt to overcome polarization in their government. Issues surrounding immigration and foreigners are contested, as are the nation's tax and bank policies. The establishment of a flexible relationship with the EU is another problem.

The Swiss have long considered theirs to be a special nation. As they continue to accommodate changes in the twenty-first century, they do so with a strong democracy and a long history of unified diversity. The Swiss seem poised to continue this trend, all while holding dear their nation's beloved natural beauty, valued traditions, and admired skills.

TIMELINE

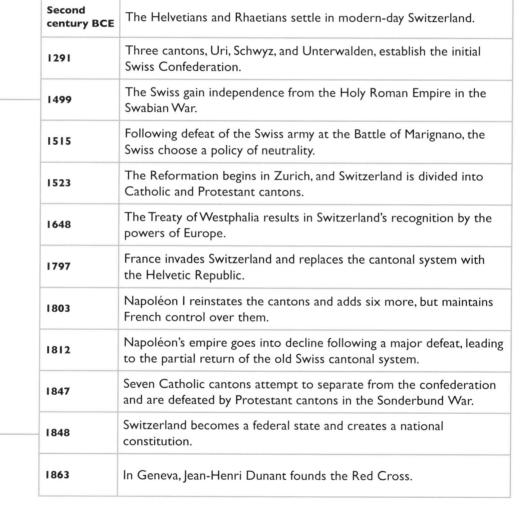

Second century BCE	The Helvetians and Rhaetians settle in modern-day Switzerland.
1291	Three cantons, Uri, Schwyz, and Unterwalden, establish the initial Swiss Confederation.
1499	The Swiss gain independence from the Holy Roman Empire in the Swabian War.
1515	Following defeat of the Swiss army at the Battle of Marignano, the Swiss choose a policy of neutrality.
1523	The Reformation begins in Zurich, and Switzerland is divided into Catholic and Protestant cantons.
1648	The Treaty of Westphalia results in Switzerland's recognition by the powers of Europe.
1797	France invades Switzerland and replaces the cantonal system with the Helvetic Republic.
1803	Napoléon I reinstates the cantons and adds six more, but maintains French control over them.
1812	Napoléon's empire goes into decline following a major defeat, leading to the partial return of the old Swiss cantonal system.
1847	Seven Catholic cantons attempt to separate from the confederation and are defeated by Protestant cantons in the Sonderbund War.
1848	Switzerland becomes a federal state and creates a national constitution.
1863	In Geneva, Jean-Henri Dunant founds the Red Cross.

1865	On July 14, Edward Whymper becomes the first person to climb the Matterhorn.
1874	Switzerland revises its constitution, strengthening the federal government and mandating education.
1914–1918	Switzerland remains neutral during World War I.
1939–1945	Switzerland remains neutral during World War II and trades with both the Allied and Axis powers.
1970	Services begin to overtake industry as the chief driver of the Swiss economy.
1989	Switzerland experiences a severe economic downturn.
1998	On August 12, Swiss banks agree to pay Holocaust survivors more than $1.25 million.
2002	Switzerland becomes a member of the United Nations.
2009	The Swiss economy is badly affected by the global economic crisis.
2010	In June, Swiss parliament approves releasing secret bank information to the US Internal Revenue Service, which wants to prosecute tax evaders.
2010	Women outnumber men in the Federal Council for the first time in Swiss history.
2012	Swiss banking secrecy and tax policies come under increasing pressure.

FACTS AT YOUR FINGERTIPS

GEOGRAPHY

Official name: Swiss Confederation, or Switzerland (in German, Schweizerische Eidgenossenschaft, or die Schweiz; in French, Confederation Suisse, or Suisse; in Italian, Confederazione Svizzera, or Svizzera; in Romansh, Confederaziun Svizra, or Svizra)

Area: 15,917 square miles (41,277 sq km)

Climate: Temperate

Highest elevation: Dufourspitze, 15,203 feet (4,634 m) above sea level

Lowest elevation: Lake Maggiore, 640 feet (195 m) above sea level

Significant geographic features: The Alps, the Jura, the Swiss plateau, Rhone River, Rhine River

PEOPLE

Population (July 2012 est.): 7,925,517

Most populous city: Zurich

Ethnic groups: German, 65 percent; French, 18 percent; Italian, 10 percent; Romansh, 1 percent; other, 6 percent (includes Serbo-Croatian, Albanian, Portuguese, and Spanish)

Percentage of residents living in urban areas: 74 percent

Life expectancy: 81.17 years at birth (world rank: 17)

Languages: German, French, Italian, Romansh

Religions: Roman Catholicism, 41.8 percent; Protestantism, 35.3 percent; Islam, 4.3 percent; unaffiliated, other, or none, 18.6 percent

GOVERNMENT AND ECONOMY

Government: federal republic

Capital: Bern

Date of adoption of current constitution: January 1, 2000

Head of state: Federal Council

Head of government: Federal Council

Legislature: Federal Assembly, consists of the Council of States and the National Council

Currency: Swiss franc

Industries and natural resources: agriculture, chemicals and pharmaceuticals, banking, tourism, food

NATIONAL SYMBOLS

Holidays: New Year's Day, Good Friday, Easter, Easter Monday, Ascension Day, National Day (August 1), Christmas Day, and Boxing Day (December 26).

Flag: A red square with a white equilateral cross in the center.

National anthem: "Schweizerpsalm" ("Swiss Psalm")

KEY PEOPLE

Julius Caesar (100–44 BCE), Roman leader who forced the Helvetians to stay on the Swiss plateau and gained control of the tribe for the Romans

Huldrych Zwingli (1484–1531), leader of the German-speaking Reformation in Switzerland

John Calvin (1509–1564), leader of the French-speaking Reformation in Switzerland

Napoléon Bonaparte (1769–1821), French leader, restored the cantonal system in 1803 and added to it

Paul Klee (1879–1940), Swiss artist and premier twentieth-century painter

Carl Jung (1875–1961), influential Swiss psychologist and psychiatrist

Jean Piaget (1896–1980), Swiss psychologist and philosopher who figured prominently in the area of developmental psychology

CANTON; CAPITAL

Aargau; Aarau

Appenzell Ausserrhoden; Herisau

Appenzell Innerrhoden; Appenzell

Basel-Landschaft; Liestal

Basel-Stadt; Basel

Bern; Bern

Fribourg; Fribourg

Geneva; Geneva

Glarus; Glarus

Graubünden; Chur

Jura; Delémont

Lucerne; Lucerne

Neuchâtel; Neuchâtel

Nidwalden; Stans

Obwalden; Sarnen

Saint Gallen; Saint Gallen

Schaffhausen; Schaffhausen

Schwyz; Schwyz

Solothurn; Solothurn

Thurgau; Frauenfeld

Ticino; Bellinzona

Uri; Altdorf

Valais; Sion

Vaud; Lausanne

Zug; Zug

Zurich; Zurich

GLOSSARY

bicameral

A legislative body with two separate chambers.

coniferous

A tree that has cones and often needles.

deciduous

A tree that loses its leaves each year.

Homo sapiens

Human beings as known today, advanced from prehistoric people.

isolationist

A policy of not getting deeply involved with other countries.

mercenary

A soldier paid to fight for another country's army.

Neolithic

The last period of the Stone Age, during which people created and used instruments of polished stone.

ogre

A mythical person-eating creature.

pharmaceutical

A product made to be used as a drug.

recession

A period of economic decline.

referendum

A vote on a particular issue or question.

subatomic

Smaller than an atom.

yodeling

A distinctive style of singing in which high notes and low notes alternate quickly.

ADDITIONAL RESOURCES

SELECTED BIBLIOGRAPHY

Fisher, Teresa. *Switzerland*. Washington, D.C.: National Geographic, 2012. Print.

Swiss Confederation. "The Swiss Confederation: A Brief Guide: 2012." Bern: SFBL, 2012. Print.

SwissWorld.org. Federal Department of Foreign Affairs, n.d. Web. 22 May 2012.

"The World Factbook: Switzerland." *Central Intelligence Agency*. Central Intelligence Agency, 3 May 2012. Web. 3 June 2012.

FURTHER READINGS

Bewes, Diccon. *Swiss Watching: Inside Europe's Landlocked Island*. London: Nicholas Brealey, 2010. Print.

Birmingham, David. *Switzerland: Village History*. Athens, OH: Swallow Press, 2004. Print.

Levy, Patricia, and Richard Levy. *Switzerland*, 2nd ed. Tarrytown, NY: Marshall Cavendish, 2005. Print.

Maycock, Kendall. *Switzerland: A Quick Guide to Customs & Etiquette*. London: Kuperard, 2006. Print.

Porter, Darwin, and Danforth Prince. *Frommer's Switzerland*, 14th ed. Hoboken, NJ: Wiley, 2010. Print.

WEB LINKS

To learn more about Switzerland, visit ABDO Publishing Company online at **www.abdopublishing.com**. Web sites about Switzerland are featured on our Book Links page. These links are routinely monitored and updated to provide the most current information available.

PLACES TO VISIT

If you are ever in Switzerland, consider checking out these important and interesting sites!

Altstadt, Bern

This medieval neighborhood of Switzerland's capital city has hundreds of sites, including churches and 250 fountains.

Saint Gottard Pass

This is a north-south pass in the Alps. Today, the area is accessible by car and train.

Swiss National Museum

The Swiss National Museum (SNM)—National Museum Zurich, the Castle of Prangins and the Forum of Swiss History Schwyz, plus collections at other locations—preserves and showcases Switzerland's history and current topics. The SNM's basic collection has approximately 1 million artifacts.

The Swiss Path

This 22-mile (36 km) hiking path located in Rütli Meadow was inaugurated in 1991 in celebration of Switzerland's seven-hundredth birthday. Along the way, visitors can see chapels and castles.

SOURCE NOTES

CHAPTER 1. A VISIT TO SWITZERLAND

1. "Info." *BärenPark Bern.* BärenPark Bern, n.d. Web. 10 Sept. 2012.
2. "Rail." *Swiss World.* Federal Department of Foreign Affairs, n.d. Web. 10 Sept. 2012.

CHAPTER 2. GEOGRAPHY: LAND OF CONTRASTS

1. "Switzerland." *Encyclopædia Britannica.* Encyclopædia Britannica, 2012. Web. 10 Sept. 2012.
2. "The World Factbook: Switzerland." *Central Intelligence Agency.* Central Intelligence Agency, 24 Aug. 2012. Web. 10 Sept. 2012.
3. "Switzerland." *Encyclopædia Britannica.* Encyclopædia Britannica, 2012. Web. 10 Sept. 2012.
4. "Alps." *Encyclopædia Britannica.* Encyclopædia Britannica, 2012. Web. 10 Sept. 2012.
5. "Jura Mountains." *Encyclopædia Britannica.* Encyclopædia Britannica, 2012. Web. 10 Sept. 2012.
6. "Matterhorn." *Encyclopædia Britannica.* Encyclopædia Britannica, 2012. Web. 10 Sept. 2012.
7. "Switzerland." *Encyclopædia Britannica.* Encyclopædia Britannica, 2012. Web. 10 Sept. 2012.
8. "Saint Gotthard Pass." *Encyclopædia Britannica.* Encyclopædia Britannica, 2012. Web. 10 Sept. 2012.
9. Ibid.
10. "The Swiss Plateau." *Swiss World.* Federal Department of Foreign Affairs, n.d. Web. 10 Sept. 2012.
11. "Water Sources." *Swiss World.* Federal Department of Foreign Affairs, n.d. Web. 10 Sept. 2012.
12. Ibid.
13. "Switzerland." *Encyclopædia Britannica.* Encyclopædia Britannica, 2012. Web. 10 Sept. 2012.
14. Ibid.
15. "Switzerland." *Weatherbase.* Canty and Associates, 2012. Web. 10 Sept. 2012.

CHAPTER 3. ANIMALS AND NATURE: ALPINE WILDLIFE

1. "Biodiversity in Switzerland." *Swiss World.* Federal Department of Foreign Affairs, n.d. Web. 10 Sept. 2012.
2. "Mountain Animals." *Swiss World.* Federal Department of Foreign Affairs, n.d. Web. 10 Sept. 2012.
3. Ibid.
4. "The Role of Forests." *Swiss World.* Federal Department of Foreign Affairs, n.d. Web. 10 Sept. 2012.
5. Theresa Fisher. *Switzerland.* Washington, DC: National Geographic, 2012. Print. 26.
6. "Melting Glaciers." *Swiss World.* Federal Department of Foreign Affairs, n.d. Web. 10 Sept. 2012.
7. "Climate Change: Flora and Fauna." *Swiss World.* Federal Department of Foreign Affairs, n.d. Web. 10 Sept. 2012.
8. "Summary Statistics: Summaries by Country, Table 5, Threatened Species in Each Country." *IUCN Red List of Threatened Species.* International Union for Conservation of Nature and Natural Resources, 2011. Web. 10 Sept. 2012.

9. "The Swiss Plateau." *Swiss World*. Federal Department of Foreign Affairs, n.d. Web. 10 Sept. 2012.

10. "Groundwater." *Swiss World*. Federal Department of Foreign Affairs, n.d. Web. 10 Sept. 2012.

11. "Switzerland." *Encyclopædia Britannica*. Encyclopædia Britannica, 2012. Web. 10 Sept. 2012.

12. "Concerns Raised Over Disappearing Species." *SwissInfo.ch*. Swiss Broadcasting Corporation, 22 May 2009. Web. 10 Sept. 2012.

CHAPTER 4. HISTORY: STRENGTH IN UNITY

1. "Swiss Guards." *Encyclopædia Britannica*. Encyclopædia Britannica, 2012. Web. 10 Sept. 2012.

2. Ibid.

3. "The Thirty Years' War." *Swiss World*. Federal Department of Foreign Affairs, n.d. Web. 10 Sept. 2012.

4. "World War II." *Encyclopædia Britannica*. Encyclopædia Britannica, 2012. Web. 10 Sept. 2012.

5. "The Swiss Economy in World War II." *Swiss World*. Federal Department of Foreign Affairs, n.d. Web. 10 Sept. 2012.

6. "The World Factbook: Switzerland." *Central Intelligence Agency*. Central Intelligence Agency, 24 Aug. 2012. Web. 10 Sept. 2012.

7. "A Chronology of Events." *Frontline: Nazi Gold*. PBS, 2012. Web. 10 Sept. 2012.

8. "US Tax Cheats Pay For Secret Swiss Accounts." *SwissInfo.ch*. Swiss Broadcasting Corporation, 3 Aug. 2010. Web. 10 Sept. 2012.

9. Sophie Douez. "Heated Debate Delivers Tax Assistance Law." *SwissInfo.ch*. Swiss Broadcasting Corporation, 29 Feb. 2012. Web. 10 Sept. 2012.

CHAPTER 5. PEOPLE: DIVERSE CULTURES COEXIST

1. "Population Size and Population Composition." *Swiss Statistics*. Swiss Confederation, 30 Aug. 2012. Web. 10 Sept. 2012.

2. "The World Factbook: Switzerland." *Central Intelligence Agency*. Central Intelligence Agency, 24 Aug. 2012. Web. 10 Sept. 2012.

3. Ibid.

4. Ibid.

5. Ibid.

6. "Minorities and Bilingualism." *Swiss World*. Federal Department of Foreign Affairs, n.d. Web. 10 Sept. 2012.

7. "The World Factbook: Switzerland." *Central Intelligence Agency*. Central Intelligence Agency, 24 Aug. 2012. Web. 10 Sept. 2012.

8. Ibid.

9. Ibid.

10. Ibid.

11. "Family Life." *Swiss World*. Federal Department of Foreign Affairs, n.d. Web. 10 Sept. 2012.

12. "The World Factbook: Switzerland." *Central Intelligence Agency*. Central Intelligence Agency, 24 Aug. 2012. Web. 10 Sept. 2012.

13. Ibid.

14. Ibid.

15. Ibid.

16. "Religious Landscape." *Swiss World*. Federal Department of Foreign Affairs, n.d. Web. 10 Sept. 2012.

17. Ibid.

18. Ibid.

19. Clare O'Dea. "Muslims in Switzerland 'Lack Legal Protection.'" *SwissInfo.ch*. Swiss Broadcasting Corporation, 24 Apr. 2012. Web. 10 Sept. 2012.

20. "Swiss Voters Back Ban On Minarets." *BBC News*. BBC, 29 Nov. 2009. Web. 10 Sept. 2012.

CHAPTER 6. CULTURE: UNITED, NOT UNIFORM

1. "Roger Federer." *Encyclopædia Britannica*. Encyclopædia Britannica, 2012. Web. 11 Sept. 2012.

2. "Football." *Swiss World*. Federal Department of Foreign Affairs, n.d. Web. 11 Sept. 2012.

3. "Large Hadron Collider (LHC)." *Encyclopædia Britannica*. Encyclopædia Britannica, 2012. Web. 11 Sept. 2012.

CHAPTER 7. POLITICS: SWISS DEMOCRACY

1. Swiss Confederation. *The Swiss Confederation: A Brief Guide*. Bern: SFBL, 2012. Print. 14.

2. Ibid. 79.

3. Ibid. 46.

4. Ibid. 17.

5. Ibid.

6. Ibid. 16.

7. Ibid.

CHAPTER 8. ECONOMICS: SERVICE FOCUSED

1. "The World Factbook: Switzerland." *Central Intelligence Agency*. Central Intelligence Agency, 24 Aug. 2012. Web. 11 Sept. 2012.

2. Ibid.

3. "Banking." *Swiss World*. Federal Department of Foreign Affairs, n.d. Web. 11 Sept. 2012.

4. "Tourism." *Swiss World*. Federal Department of Foreign Affairs, n.d. Web. 11 Sept. 2012.

5. Ibid.

6. "Companies." *Swiss World*. Federal Department of Foreign Affairs, n.d. Web. 11 Sept. 2012.

7. "The World Factbook: Switzerland." *Central Intelligence Agency*. Central Intelligence Agency, 24 Aug. 2012. Web. 11 Sept. 2012.

8. Ibid.

9. "Switzerland." *Encyclopædia Britannica*. Encyclopædia Britannica, 2012. Web. 11 Sept. 2012.

10. "Farming Facts and Figures." *Swiss World*. Federal Department of Foreign Affairs, n.d. Web. 11 Sept. 2012.

11. Ibid.

12. "Rail." *Swiss World*. Federal Department of Foreign Affairs, n.d. Web. 11 Sept. 2012.

13. "Mobility." *Swiss World*. Federal Department of Foreign Affairs, n.d. Web. 11 Sept. 2012.

14. Ibid.

15. "Hydroelectricity." *Swiss World*. Federal Department of Foreign Affairs, n.d. Web. 11 Sept. 2012.

16. "Switzerland." *Internet World Stats*. Miniwatts Marketing Group, 2012. Web. 11 Sept. 2012.

17. "The World Factbook: Switzerland." *Central Intelligence Agency*. Central Intelligence Agency, 24 Aug. 2012. Web. 11 Sept. 2012.

18. Ibid.

19. Ibid.

20. Ibid.

21. Ibid.

CHAPTER 9. SWITZERLAND TODAY

1. "Home and Work." *Swiss World*. Federal Department of Foreign Affairs, n.d. Web. 11 Sept. 2012.

2. "Television." *SSG SSR*. Swiss Broadcasting Corporation, n.d. Web. 11 Sept. 2012.

3. "Swiss Education System." *SwissInfo.ch*. Swiss Broadcasting Corporation, 3 Feb. 2011. Web. 11 Sept. 2012.

4. "Air: Impact on Health." *Swiss World*. Federal Department of Foreign Affairs, n.d. Web. 11 Sept. 2012.

5. "Household Waste." *Swiss World*. Federal Department of Foreign Affairs, n.d. Web. 11 Sept. 2012.

6. "Farming: Current Challenges." *Swiss World*. Federal Department of Foreign Affairs, n.d. Web. 11 Sept. 2012.

7. Theresa Fisher. *Switzerland*. Washington, D.C.: National Geographic, 2012. Print. 38.

INDEX

PHOTO CREDITS